Table of Contents

D1160956

Preface

I have been most fortunate in having a rather unusual and interesting life; consequently my family and many of my friends have urged me to commit details of my life and background to a written document.

In this booklet I have started, in Section One, an autobiography of my life.

In Section Two, I provide information about my Dad, Alexander Nikolaevich Jedenoff, and the Jedenoff family history. There then follows a description of my mother, Varvara (Barbara) Vasilievna, and history of her family, the Sepiagin Family.

In Section Three, there is a description of my wife Barbara's history and her paternal "Family of Cull". Then follows the history of her mother, Georgina Henninger Cull and of the Henninger Family.

Section Four contains the Appendix which lists some vignettes of my life and provides some testimonials.

In writing this work, I have been encouraged and helped by many people and for this I am very appreciative. My special thanks go to former curator of the Stanford Hoover Institute, Elena Danielson, PhD; Harriet Wallis, author of many sports articles in the Inter-mountain area and a "Wild Old Bunch of Alta" spokesperson; Bobbie Dodson-Nielsen, a close friend and contributing author to several publications in the Orinda area; my son, Nick Jedenoff, for editing; my granddaughter, Stephanie Billett, for advice and technical assistance; Joe Billett, my son-in-law, for help in publishing the original manuscript; and to my friend Tom Scovel for help in rewriting the original edition into this version adapted for publishing. Finally, I am deeply indebted to my new friend, Adam Engst, CEO of the popular Apple website TidBITS, for reformatting this manuscript for a more attractive appearance when published in digital form.

SECTION ONE
My Odyssey

Chapter 1: My Early Years

Petrozavodsk, Russia, a city you probably have never heard of, is where I came into this world on July 5, 1917 (June 22, according to the Julian calendar used in Russia at that time). This ancient city located on Lake Onega, approximately 260 miles northeast of St. Petersburg, was selected and renamed by Czar Peter the Great, in 1703, to be an arsenal and a foundry to make cannons and other armaments which were needed to support Russia's war with Sweden.

Later, it became the the capital of the Republic of Karelia and the section headquarters for the railroad running from St. Petersburg to the northern seaport of Murmansk.

My Dad in his office in Petrozavodsk, 1917

My father, Alexander Nikolaevich Jedenoff, was stationed here with the railroad in the capacity of "Revisor Dvazhenia" (literally translated as Inspector of operations). Both of my parents were members of the Russian nobility (see below for details). When the Bolsheviks seized power in Saint Petersburg on November 7, 1917, four months after my birth, my family, which resided close to this insurrection, was in great jeopardy, so they decided to move to a safer location, further from the center of violent Bolshevik atrocities.

On September 1, 1918, my father was transferred to the Perm Railroad administration in Ekaterinburg located on the border with Siberia, and in July 1919, he became the inspector of the Ural region. Later in 1919, in order to get his family still further away from the spreading revolution, my father received permission to move his family to Harbin, Manchuria. This required traveling on the Trans-Siberian railroad to Vladivostok in eastern Russia (Siberia). This was the route of many "White Russians" who were fleeing the "Red" Bolshevik forces.

Initially, we had the convenience of a private railroad car, assigned to my father because of his position with the railroad. As we traveled through the war zone, the private car was confiscated because of the greater need for more rolling stock by our Loyalist military forces.

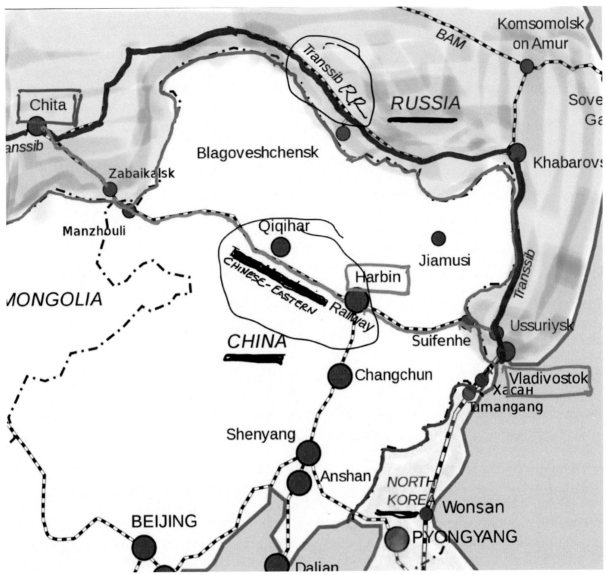

Alternate routes between Chita Siberia (Russia) and Vladivostok via Trans-Siberian RR (shown in purple) and the much shorter Chinese Eastern RR (shown in red).

Travel across Siberia proved to be quite hazardous, as our train was captured by the Bolsheviks and then rescued by the Loyalist (White) forces on several occasions. In this back and forth process, most of our valuables were confiscated. Finally, we made it to Vladivostok.

In early 1920, my father was assigned as Assistant Superintendent of the ChineseEastern Railroad and the family moved to Harbin, Manchuria (China). Harbin was the Headquarters of that Railroad which was built and owned by Russia and operated on land leased from China. This Railroad was built in the late 1890's and early 1900's and connected Vladivostok with Chita in Siberia, and ran on a relatively flat roadbed, in contrast to the relatively unstable path of the Trans-Siberian railroad along the Amur River. It played a very important part in the revolution. Armaments, supplies, and troops arriving in Vladivostok, the principal port on the East Coast of

Siberia, were transported to the front by means of this Railroad.

After the collapse of the White Forces, the Jedenoff family considered emigrating to the USA. In May of 1921, my mother, accompanied by my brother and me, traveled to California for a four-month visit to investigate the possibility of settling in America. Upon our return, later in 1921, the Jedenoffs applied for immigration and, subsequently, came to Seattle, Washington on board the SS President Jackson, arriving on March 3, 1923.

On September 28, 1928, all four members of the Jedenoff family were granted U.S. Citizenship.

I was enrolled in elementary school in 1923 attending St. Joseph Grammar School (a private Catholic School). Unfamiliarity with the English language made the initial education difficult, and I had to repeat the first year. In 1926 I was transferred to Lowell Grammar School (a public school), in the Capitol Hill district of Seattle. I received my diploma from that school in 1932. While in Seattle, I was active in the Cub Scouts, and later the Boy Scouts. I received my Eagle Scout award in 1932, and was the youngest person to receive such an award in the Seattle Council as of that time.

Adjustment to life in America was difficult for our family. The problem of learning a new language and accepting such extreme changes in the family's social and economic status placed great stress on my parent's relationship. Consequently, my father and mother separated in 1930 and were later divorced, with my Mom being awarded custody over me, while my Dad retained custody of my older brother, Alexis. In 1932 my mother moved to California and settled in San Leandro, where I was enrolled in the San Leandro Junior High School. She married George Ivanovich Shishko, also an immigrant, who had served in the Russian White army during the Revolution and was decorated for valor with the St. George Cross. The transition to life in America was also difficult for him, especially during the depth of the depression. He obtained employment as a laborer and concrete finisher working on the huge San Francisco Hetch Hetchy water project. In 1934, his work on the project was completed and his employment came to end, making it necessary for him to find work elsewhere.

To minimize living expenses it was decided that our family would move to San Francisco and would share an apartment with Mr. Shishko's mother, sister, and brother-in-law. This was not a very happy arrangement and caused considerable tension. The apartment was located in the Sunset District, and I was enrolled in Polytechnic High School which was located just a few blocks away. Mr. Shishko picked up whatever work was available sometimes working only 5 of 6 days a month. Money problems contributed to the tension, and so my mother, an accomplished pianist, supplemented the family income by providing private piano lessons to the few children who could afford to pay for them during those hard times. However, my mother always made sure that my basic needs received top priority, and occasionally this resulted in intense family arguments.

The living arrangement was pretty tight, but a tiny walk-in closet was converted into a study so that I was able to have some privacy for my home work.

Having three families in one small flat sharing a single bathroom proved almost unbearable and my family ultimately moved to a separate small apartment. In order to save money, two more moves were made during the period of two years. In spite of these difficulties, and with encouragement from my mother, I was able to get good grades in school.

I was an honor student and earned athletic awards in football, swimming and track. I received my diploma in December of 1935 and served as class valedictorian. I applied and was accepted to Stanford University, hoping to receive an athletic scholarship, having played quarterback on the Polytechnic City Championship football team.

Art Wells (R) and me graduating from Polytechnic HS, December 1935

Chapter 2: Stanford University

During the six months prior to enrollment at Stanford, I tried to get temporary employment, but since this was during the depth of the depression, jobs just were not available. In order to use my time productively, I enrolled in the San Francisco Junior College. This was only the second year of this newly organized institution, and it had no facilities of its own. Morning classes were held at the sparse California Extension building on Powell Street, and afternoon classes (for those of us in pre-engineering) were held across town at Galileo High School. For transportation, we made extensive use of streetcars and cable cars at five cents a ride, though we often saved the fare by riding outside on the "cowcatchers" of the street cars.

During this time, I attended classes with my high school buddy, Art Wells, who was also interested in pursuing an engineering career. In the fall of 1936 we parted company, but remained close friends. Art enrolled at UC Berkeley while I enrolled at Cal's arch-rival, Stanford. Art and I attended Big Games together, although Art had the greater pleasure since Cal won all four football games during our undergraduate years.

In early 1936, the depression was still in the full force and my stepfather was out of work. The family ran out of money and could not afford rent even for the modest apartment in which we were living. In order to have a roof over our heads we had to move again. The cheapest place we could find was an unfinished basement area in the back of a San Francisco flat a single room with a sloping floor, partially paved and partially dirt. The sewer lines for the upstairs living areas ran uncovered overhead. There was one bathroom, running water and a make shift arrangement for cooking. It was a real hovel, but my wonderful mother tried her best to make it feel like home. She put a carpet over the unpaved floor, hung sheets across the single room in order to partition off the space to simulate individual rooms.

What an experience for someone who had been brought up in the lap of luxury! The address was 1029 and one-half Fell Street an address and an experience never to be forgotten.

In the Spring of 1936, in connection with my request for a scholarship, I was interviewed by members of the Stanford Alumni Association. Jack Rice, a feisty little guy and Chairman of the Hercules Powder Company, sized me up and stated he thought I was pretty small to be a football player. Then he looked me in the eye and queried, "have you got any guts? Are you willing to work?

I replied affirmatively to both pointed questions not really being sure. Jack Rice consequently arranged for me to have a summer job at the Bald Eagle Mines of the California Chemical Corp., located about an hour's drive (over a rustic dirt road) out of Gustine, CA. This was a magnesite mine and the work involved pick-and-shovel activity in an under ground mine. The pay was fifty cents per hour. Because of its remote location, it was necessary to live in company barracks and to pay out $1.50 a day for room and board. The mine operated 6 days a week with off days, back to back.

Since there was nothing else to do on days off, I and another college prospect who was also receiving summer employment were given the opportunity to work during those days, performing maintenance and cleanup duties, and thus obtaining additional earnings.

The seasoned miners looked upon us two kids as their charges. Although the miners engaged in nightly poker and wine drinking, we were not permitted to do any of such things. We got some tremendous lectures and all kinds of advice, all directed toward "making something of our lives." An eighteen-year-old kid just couldn't get any better motivation. I developed a lasting friendship with the other summer worker, Paul Durckel who had played football for Oakland Tech High School and was also admitted into Stanford.

George at the entrance to Bald Eagle mine, 1936

Late that summer, I received a polite letter from Stanford informing me that "because of inadequate funds" I would not be granted a scholarship at that time. The letter, however encouraged me to enroll, nonetheless, and to finance my tuition through the use of favorable interest loans. In order to pay my school expenses, Stanford would assist me in obtaining part-time employment. By the end of that previous summer, I had accumulated $250. At Stanford, tuition and fees alone were $345 for the year. Thus, I received my first lesson in deficit financing.

In the meantime, my stepfather finally obtained a steady job as custodian, working for the city of San Francisco at the airport. In time, my parents were able to scrape enough money together to make a downpayment on a new tract house being built on the sand flats in Western San Francisco by the Dolger Construction Co. These were lowcost homes, but a great improvement over the rental units which we previously occupied.

I arrived on the Stanford Campus in early Sept. of 1936 to participate in two weeks of football training camp prior to the start of classes. Although the varsity players were provided with free room and board, the Freshmen did not receive such benefits. In order to provide for meals during this time, I obtained a job at the Sunset Cafeteria in downtown Palo Alto. I was made assistant to a Filipino dishwasher. There was no cash received, but I was provided meals for my services. Unfortunately, after several hours in the hot steaming atmosphere of the dishwasher, and participating in scraping "slop" off of the dishes, all signs of appetite disappeared. After four days of work with no desire to eat any of the food for which I was compensated, it was clear that this was a losing proposition and I quit.

When classes finally began, I was engaged as a "hasher" (waiter) at Roble Hall, the frosh girl's dormitory. I also earned fifty cents an hour supported by The National Youth Administration (federal aid) jobs such as cleaning up the athletic locker room and working at the library. With this heavy schedule while being enrolled in engineering (with its required labs), I found that trying to make the frosh football squad was almost impossible. The team had considerable talent, and the prospect of getting a starting position seemed quite remote. What made it difficult was that by the time it was my opportunity to participate in scrimmage in order to show what I could do, it was necessary for me to leave the field just in time to make it for my hashing job. The manager of resident dining at Roble Hall was a capable but tough cookieMrs. Sterling was her name, and low and behold, a decade or so later, she was the University's "first lady," when her husband, Wally Sterling, was selected as president of Stanford!

Phi Kappa Psi Fraternity House

During winter quarter of my freshman year, I went out for Rugby and found that I was suited better for that sport. I played in all of the varsity games, and started and played the entire Big Game against UC that year. In the Spring I pledged the Phi Kappa Psi fraternity and was assured of getting a hashing job, in the house, during my sophomore year. My study efforts paid off, and I received excellent grades, and as a result was awarded a George Gamble scholarship for the following year. This was the most lucrative scholarship available at that time and it paid $600 per year more than enough to pay for tuition and books.

During the summer of 1937, I got a job as a roustabout with the Ohio Oil Co. (now Marathon Oil Co.) in Bakersfield, CA. I was involved in the construction of pipelines and maintenance of oil wells, along with some well-drilling activity. The work was hard, the summer heat in Bakersfield was extreme (reaching 115 degrees), but the pay was good almost double of what I had earned the previous summer working underground in the mines.

My sophomore year proved to be a lot less difficult. Thanks to my scholarship award, my summer earnings, and my hashing job at the Phi Psi house, my financial situation was much improved. I continued to get excellent grades in the engineering program and played on the varsity Rugby team.

The summer of 1938 was a different story. Due to a setback in the economic recovery that year, summer employment proved difficult to obtain. I worked for one month as a counselor in a boys camp in the Santa Cruz Mountains, at very minimal pay. Then I worked as a shipping clerk at the Jim Wylie (Pear) Packing plant in Santa Clara. Jim Wylie, a legendary rugby star of the New Zealand "All-blacks", was the volunteer rugby coach at Stanford.

That fall, the Phi Psi's elected me house manager. I kept the accounts, collected the monthly room and board bills, paid all fraternity bills, supervised the staff of two cooks and a houseboy, and made sure the fraternity chapter was not losing money. It was wonderful experience as well as helpful in support of my education.

The summer of 1939 was more rewarding. I got a summer job with the Ohio Oil Co. at its main Lincoln Refinery in Robinson, Ill. I was employed as a junior engineer in the erection of a Kellogg Cracking Unit at the refinery, and I worked closely with two experienced field engineers. Living in a small town was quite an experience as well. I did all the surveying, worked with the foundation crews, and performed miscellaneous

In Bakersfield with the Ohio oil company, summer of 1937

Working in the house manager's office

engineering assignments. It was a fun job. We worked long hours which the summer daylight permitted, and at the end of the day, we three engineers would go to a local pub where we would roll the dice to see who would pay for the beer, which at that time was only five cents a glass. After a long day in the summer heat, a glass of beer was a pleasant reward.

While we were relaxing in the pub we planned the next day's activities. The two engineers were from Fort Worth, Texas and were great guys and taught me a lot about the practical aspects of engineering. The Manager of the refinery was pleased with my work and offered me permanent employment, once I got my degree.

At the end of summer and just prior to returning to Stanford, I met my Dad in Ohio, and together we traveled to New York to visit the World's Fair. 1939 was a historic year for world fairs because simultaneously world fairs were being held in both New York and San Francisco. Treasure Island was created by dredging the Bay specifically for staging the Fair at that location. During the fall of that year another historic event took place with dire consequences for the world: Hitler marched into Poland an event which precipitated World War II.

The fall of 1939 was a busy time for me for this was my senior year. I continued as house manager and still maintained my Gamble Scholarship. I still played rugby and had the opportunity to compete on an all-star team at the San Francisco World's Fair. I maintained excellent grades and was elected president of Tau Beta Pi, the national honorary engineering fraternity. In that capacity I was a delegate to the national conference, held in Columbia, MO another great experience for a young man.

I completed my senior year and graduated in June of 1940, Magna Cum Laude. (42 such honors out of a total of 814 Bachelor of Arts degrees conferred). I was elected into Phi Beta Kappa, national scholarship society. Scholastically, I graduated second in my class in the School of Engineering.

However, I felt that I needed additional education. I applied for the Degree of Engineer (Masters Degree), but wished to take available elective courses in the Graduate School of Business.

During the summer of 1940, I accepted a job with Columbia Steel Company, a subsidiary of U.S. Steel Corporation, in its wire-rope works, located on 17th and Folsom Streets in San Francisco. This was a longstanding operation and, among other things, had made most of the cables for the San Francisco cable cars. Experience at this firm proved to be instrumental in shaping my future career. I was assigned as a staff assistant to Donald E. Rice, newly appointed manager of the Rope Mill. Don, an Ohio State engineer, had extensive experience in the Worchester Rope Mill in New Jersey and was given the task of modernizing the facilities and of directing the relocation of these facilities to Columbia Steel's plant in Pittsburg, CA. I thoroughly enjoyed the work and the challenges involved and decided I would direct my future development toward an operating position. This would provide me with the opportunity of using my technical education as well as to work more closely with people. On the strength of this decision, I modified my scholastic plans; rather than seeking a Master's degree in engineering I decided to pursue an MBA Degree at the Stanford Graduate School of Business, majoring in Production Management.

Financially, attending graduate school was yet another challenge. I no longer had the opportunity to enjoy a lucrative scholarship and was no longer eligible to serve as house manager of the Phi Psi house. Through previous contacts, I was able to obtain a "hashing" job for my meals at the Chi Omega Sorority and earn some income through part time employment in the library. For my tuition I was able to obtain a loan.

During the fall quarter I secured a room at Dean Hugh Jackson's home a room he made available to one of his students in exchange for some menial tasks around the house and for dusting off his black Packard every morning. In attending the Graduate School of Business (GSB), I quickly discovered that it required a complete change in study habits and content from the previous discipline of engineering.

That fall, while hashing at the Chi Omega Sorority, I met a cute little sophomore, from Douglas, AZ., named Barbara Cull. I knew from the start that she was the one with whom I wanted to spend the rest of my life. She was not so sure about that, however. Besides, she had a high school boy friend at home. A carefully thought-out aggressive plan was developed to win her over. And that is another long, but happy story.

During winter quarter I rented a cheap room in the basement of Encina Hall, and for recreation I continued to play Rugby on the Stanford varsity.

For the summer of 1941, I got employment with Standard Oil Co. of Calif. (Now Chevron Corp.) in the San Francisco Headquarters Office. I was assigned to the Economic Cost Planning Division, and had some interesting research assignments which were directed for use by the Board of Directors. I was able to live at home (in S.F.) and commute via municipal street cars to work.

Initially, the assignment appeared to be quite glamorous, but in time the daily wearing of a suit and tie, and working in the impersonal and "rarefied" atmosphere of Headquarters, convinced me I was better suited to the challenges of an operating job in the steel industry.

Fall quarter of 1941 had its challenges. Although America was not yet at war, many students, who were members of the ROTC or had acquired reserve status, were called in for active duty. Finances were tight, and I had to rent a cheap "room", which was actually a converted chicken coop, from Miss Lillian Owens, a faculty member of the GSB. Fortunately, I didn't have to live in that unit very long.

At the conclusion of the previous scholastic year, at graduation time, the Alpha Delta Phi fraternity got into serious trouble. It's graduating seniors decided to celebrate a little too vigorously, and the fraternity got kicked off the campus. After some intensive negotiations that summer, the underclassmen were permitted to return to the house, under probation, and under the watchful eye of a "responsible" graduate student, appointed by the Dean of Men. This person was to live in the house and insure responsible behavior a sort of a male "housemother". Such a person, Joe Weiner, was chosen but in October, he was called in by his draft board. I applied and was selected by the Dean's office as a replacement. This turned out to be a great assignment free room and board position of authority at the head of the table with the task of having the fraternity officers fulfill their responsibility of keeping things under control. No tattletale reports to the Dean were required, so long as things were kept under control. Fortunately, all involved made mighty sure that order prevailed.

December of 1941 proved to be a most significant month. On the night of December 6, while on a date with Barbara, I made a formal proposal of marriage, and Barbara accepted. Both of us were up on "cloud nine"! However, when I woke up the next morning the radio was blasting the news that the Japanese had just made a surprise attack on the American fleet and air force stationed at Pearl Harbor and Oahu in Hawaii. The following day, President Roosevelt declared war on Japan! This event affected the lives of almost every person on earth!

Most students who were on military reserve status or who were deemed by their draft boards to be available were immediately called into active military service. Generally, upper-class students in certain disciplines such as engineering, medicine, and science; and students in graduate school who had less than a year to complete their studies were given draft deferments.

During the previous October, I had accepted a job in the Industrial Engineering Dept. of Columbia Steel Co., but was permitted to finish the remaining six months for an MBA degree. In January, I submitted my application for a commission in the U.S. Naval Reserve, to be effective on graduation in June of 1942.

Chapter 3: After Graduation

After receiving my MBA degree, and awaiting my call to active duty with the USNR, I reported for work as an Industrial Engineer at the Pittsburg Works of Columbia (USS) Steel. I rented a room in Pittsburg in the residence of a lab technician and arranged to have my meals in a boarding house run by "old lady" Myrtle Bassett.

I was assigned, along with another engineer, to make a method's study and set incentive rates on a (reinforcing) "barbending" operation, but our research indicated that there was no way this operation could prove to be profitable, without considerable new investment, so the plant decided to discontinue that product line. While making the study, I became acquainted with the foreman of that operation a nice guy with minimal education. I was appalled that this man was earning over $250 a month, while my salary was only $125. This convinced me to drop industrial engineering and get into operations!

Shortly thereafter there was an opening in operations for a Staff Assistant to Superintendent Phil Shoenberger of the Rolling Mill Department. Phil was a very likable "old timer" who had previously served as a machinist and master mechanic in central maintenance. He detested all the administrative tasks of managing a department; consequently, my job as Staff Assistant was to perform these duties which included scheduling and holding operating and safety meetings, investigating all accidents, equipment delays, and production interruptions and analyzing the monthly cost statements and preparing variance analyses. I also indoctrinated new employees hired by the department, and performed many other miscellaneous duties. It was great experience, thanks to Phil's dislike for such tasks!

Phil drove an old Packard with a straight-sixteen engine that made the car as long as a locomotive. He just loved that car and paid more attention to it than to operating the Rolling Mills.

In late 1942, the plant was completing the installation of a new Morgan Continuous Rod Mill which was to replace the old Garrett hand mill that had been making rods for the wire mill from the early beginning. The old rod mill had low capacity, but was operated at a very high performance level. The head Roller of that mill, who was paid on a production incentive basis, was reputed to be the highest paid person in the whole plant. Because of the huge demand for steel during wartime, it was not possible to shut down the old mill while breaking in the new mill, so management decided to utilize available non-operating personnel (engineers, administrative people, etc.) to form the start-up crew assigned to operating and debugging the new rod mill. There were lots of problems that had to be worked out before the regular production crews from the old mill could be transferred to the new mill.

Elliott Peck, my predecessor as Staff Assistant, was assigned to the Morgan Rod Mill, hence the opening in the Rolling Mill Dept. Startup activity was most demanding often requiring 16-hour days of hard physical work. In about 6 months, Elliott, who was on the "heavy" side, had lost so much weight that for health reasons he was returned to his old job, and I was then assigned as his replacement on the rod mill crew. I was assigned as the "Cobble Bundler operator" with the duty of clearing the mill of "cobbles" which was rod material that had failed to proceed properly through the designated route, and would stream out, any which way. Mill difficulties often resulted in more product that failed to roll properly than that which proceeded correctly, through all the roll-stands, to the "coilers". The cobbles were red hot ribbons of steel which had to be grabbed with a hook and pulled over to a "cobble-bundler" while the steel was traveling at high speed. A most gruesome task but I was young and athletic and managed to handle this dangerous job without an injury.

Gradually, mill problems were resolved and an ever decreasing number of cobbles was generated. While I was engaged in this activity, I was notified that my Navy orders for active duty were to arrive at any time. Barbara was in her senior year at Stanford, and she and I had planned to be married in June, after she completed her scheduled graduation. Because of the obvious uncertainty concerning our immediate future, we decided to accelerate our wedding date and agreed on February 27. My boss said he would give us that week end off so we could get married.

We were wed in the Stanford Chapel on February 27, 1943, and drove to the La Playa Hotel in Carmel for our short honeymoon. On a suggestion from the departmental secretary, I sent a wire from Carmel saying that I had "car trouble" and would be late

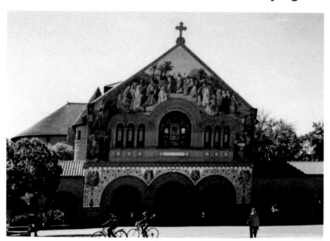

Stanford Chapel, 1943

getting back thus we squeezed out an extra day for the honeymoon. We drove back to Stanford that Monday so Barbara could take her final exams that week. After successfully completing her exams and because of extra units she had earned, she was eligible to graduate at the end of that quarter, winter quarter.

The following weekend I moved Barbara to my one-room apartment in Pittsburg and awaited orders from the Navy.

Chapter 4: Navy Service in WWII

About 3 weeks later, in March of 1943, I received orders to report for indoctrination to Naval Air Station (NAS) Quonset Point, RI. Barbara decided to travel with me and to stay close to the base, hoping to get a job in that area while I was in training. We newlyweds traveled by train to Providence, RI., arriving the day before Easter. There were absolutely no regular accommodations available, but through the USO we were sent to a private home which provided a spare mattress in their basement. So at least we had a roof over our heads. The following Monday we found a rental room for Barbara in a private home in East Greenwich, not far from the NAS.

On our way to NAS Quonset point, RI, March 1943

I reported to the base and Barbara found employment in the jewelry dept. of the Cherry & Webb Dept. store in Providence. We were disappointed, however to learn that I was not permitted to leave the base while undergoing intensive training. Although a commissioned officer, while in training I was not permitted to wear my bar or show any indication of rank.

This was like boot camp, demerits were assigned and extra duty was frequently given as punishment. During the entire training period I got only one weekend off, but occasionally was able to visit with Barbara by talking through a chain-link fence which surrounded the base. I was selected as the "company commander" and completed my training with few demerits.

On completion of training, the student officers were given permanent "billets", or orders to report for duty. Presumably because of my production background, I was assigned to the Office of Inspector of Naval Aircraft (INA), at the Douglas Aircraft Plant in El Segundo, CA. where the Navy's key airplane, the SBD dive-bomber was being made. There were many production problems, and material

SBD Dive Bomber off on a mission

shortages kept the production rate below expectations. The INA office was aggressively working with Douglas to resolve these problems.

Capt. Helber, USN, was in charge, and the production section, to which I was assigned, was headed by a very sharp ex-banker, T.P. Coats, Lt., USNR. This was a great assignment with some interesting challenges. In addition to working on the production problems, I was assigned to follow two research projects for the US Navy, and to submit weekly reports on developments and progress being made. One such project, the "Turbodyne", was being researched by Northrop Aircraft, and was the initial effort to develop a turboprop, forerunner of today's jet engine.

We rented a small house in Inglewood, close to the El Segundo aircraft plant. I found my assignment to be satisfying, however, at age 27 and healthy, I felt uncomfortable working "stateside" while most of my peers were serving overseas. After a few months I requested Capt. Helber for an overseas billet, but the Captain would not permit it, insisting that I was needed where I was. Finally, after a year, Capt. Helber was promoted to a bigger assignment. He called in each of his staff and thanked them for their support. He was very complimentary to me and thanked me for my excellent performance. This was then an opportunity for me to ask him, "If I did such a good job for you, Captain, why don't you honor my request for sea duty?" Capt. Helber weakened his stance and said "okay."

"Sea Duty" came gradually in steps. I finally received orders to report to the Naval Air Station, Pearl Harbor (Ford Island) and was assigned to the Assembly and Repair (A&R) Department where aircraft engines were repaired, usually after they had received a cable-stop "crash-barrier" landing on a carrier. This department also handled the loading of airplanes, mostly SBD Douglas dive bombers, onto Kaiser "Jeep" carriers for transfer to advanced bases.

While performing this duty I ran into a lot of old friends: Commander V.C.Finch who had been one of my engineering professors, Lt. Frank Hayward, a friend from the Stanford GSB, Lt. Frankie Albert (All American quarterback from Stanford and a rugby teammate), Rose Bowl Stanford-great Alf Brandon, and many others.

I received some challenging assignments such as developing a production planning program for the repair facilities and performing some "industrial engineering" studies.

For recreation, I went out for the Ford Island football team. Most of the team consisted of enlisted personnel, along with six or eight officers. Since on the field, rank did not count, the enlisted personnel delighted in "roughing it up" with the officers, and it got pretty darned rough at times. Several of the officers found it more than they wanted to put up with and dropped out; only two of us remained on the squad. After a while the sailors got tired of beating up on the officers, and we became one squad. I played quarterback on a rather mediocre team. Our toughest match was with the Air force at Hickam field a team which included four All-Americans. The game was more like a track meet with the Air force doing all the running, but it was a "character-building" experience. There were some great guys on the Navy team, including an excellent

Black tackle, who graduated from a Southern Black college, and was serving as a mess steward. Unfortunately, Blacks had few opportunities in the Navy in those days. He and I developed a great friendship.

But "sea duty" was disappointing because Hawaii was hardly "an advanced base" too close to city life (Honolulu) but too far from home and Barbara. Because of crowded conditions in town, with so many ships coming in for R & R, we were allowed liberty in town just two days a month. One very unpleasant assignment we drew occasionally was to serve on shore patrol duty in the city of Honolulu. We were required to wander around the bars to detect any sailors who were "out of line," improperly attired, who failed to salute an officer properly, etc. Most of these sailors had been out at sea for long periods of time and were looking forward to relaxing on shore leave.

What made it bad was that we were assigned quotas for picking up a certain number of infractions. If we failed to meet the quota, we would have to repeat the assignment. It was all pretty disgusting.

George Jedenoff inspecting the finished product – 175 gallon droppable fuel tanks

While in Hawaii, I ran into a Stanford classmate, Bill Leckie, who was assigned to a special unit formed to construct and operate a plant for the assembly of 175-gallon "droppable" fuel tanks for Naval aircraft. These "belly" tanks were very much in demand because they served to extend the range of carrier aircraft in combat. In addition, when filled with a mixture of napalm and gasoline they made very lethal incendiary bombs. It was the Navy's plan to erect a drop-tank plant closer to where the action was. Our forces had just captured the Marianas from the Japanese, and the plans were to install a drop tank plant on Guam. Bill needed an engineering officer, and I received orders to join his unit. After some initial training, the necessary equipment was provided and a unit consisting of some five officers and 120 enlisted men (all Navy craft and technical personnel) was dispatched to Guam.

The location was to be on the Orote Peninsula, adjacent to the airstrip that was being enlarged and repaired from the effects of the bombing during the invasion. Of coincidental interest, my brother, Alexis, made a landing at this precise area with the Marine Corp. during the Allied invasion of Guam. The Navy construction Battalion (C.B.'s) performed the physical erection of the plant facilities and a better bunch of competent, industrious, and cooperative people just didn't exist anyplace. Needless to say it was a real joy to work with them and the plant was constructed in record time.

Shortly after the plant was built Bill Leckie was reassigned to another billet, and I was placed in charge of the plant. We went through the startup operations successfully and were in full production on a one-shift basis. About that time the Army Air Force became aware of our plant and wanted some of the drop-tanks for their own use. The Navy was not willing to agree to this because it needed all the tanks it could make. Finally, a compromise was reached: the Navy would add on a second-shift if the Army provided the required personnel. Manpower in the Pacific was extremely tight during the war, so the Army put out directives to their many advanced bases ordering a certain number of men from each base. When so ordered, it was natural for the base commanders to release the personnel they least desired. Thus our plant received a contingent of 100 soldiers consisting of the dregs from each outpost. In charge of this muddled group was a young, "smart-assed" second lieutenant who was obsessed with his own importance. Since these new men were not technically skilled as were our Navy personnel, it was necessary to juggle the crews around. Navy personnel were assigned as supervisors or crew leaders on both crews and had the responsibility of training the soldiers to perform the production processes correctly.

A problem developed when the Army Lieutenant started injecting himself in the operations. After a heated discussion I ordered the lieutenant to get out and stay out of the plant. I then declared that all operations were to be under Navy command whether the men were army or navy and that the lieutenant was to have absolutely nothing to say in this matter. Once the men left the plant site they were then under Army command. The lieutenant. was not happy with my decision, but that's the way it operated.

While on Guam, our drop-tank facility was placed under the administrative control of Aviation Repair and Overhaul Unit Number Four (AROU #4) which was equipped with shops and other infrastructures (power plant, galley facilities, reefers for food, transportation equipment, etc.). Our living accommodations were located at the end of the airstrip on Orote Peninsula and consisted of Quonset huts with four officers to a unit. Compared to the Army that insisted on being battle ready and on keeping all personnel hardened by avoiding luxuries and required sleeping on cots, the Navy provided its personnel with beds containing springs and mattresses. Navy enlisted personnel also enjoyed similar comfortable bedding.

One of my roommates was Lt. Bob Sissler, a maintenance officer with AROU 4 who, by coincidence had worked closely with Columbia Steel Co. in Pittsburg, CA. Bob had been an engineer with Coast Industrial Gas Co. which sold natural gas to the steel mill. On Guam, Bob and I became close friends and worked out together to keep in shape. We astounded others when we played "kick goal" during the noon hour in the tropical heat, and some even questioned our sanity.

My other roommate was the medical officer assigned to the unit, Dr. Swift, whose name certainly did not reflect his personality. The tropical weather seemed to affect the doctor and he had a habit of taking numerous naps to the extent that he was referred to as "Sacky Swift." A rat infestation developed on our peninsula and Sacky was appointed as the sanitation officer to dispose of the rat problem. There was no action in this regard until one afternoon while taking his nap, Sacky woke up to find a rat crawling on his arm and staring him in the face. Needless to say we suddenly got a lot of action in a hurry!

When my contingent first arrived on Guam, the conditions were still pretty unsettled. Since the island was mostly of volcanic origin, it contained many caves where pockets of enemy Japanese were still holding out. There were occasional skirmishes, and it was most evident that hostile enemy was present because garbage containers were regularly raided for food. Some of the Japanese were so well hidden and so isolated that even several years after the war was officially over they were still hiding out.

With my friend, Capt. George Parker,USMC (R) on Guam

Life on Guam was busy, but rewarding. Hours were long and the plant operated six days a week on a two-shift basis. On Sundays I loaded up my jeep with fellow officers and we drove to another base on the island which had religious services conducted by an enthusiastic and optimistic Navy Chaplain. Sundays permitted excursions to interesting places on the beautiful island of Guam. A Stanford business school classmate of mine, Capt. George Parker, USMC, was stationed on Guam and the two of us made a number of visits to remote areas, probably against better judgment.

While on Guam, I ran into a number of friends and relatives. My only brother, Alexis, stayed on Guam for a couple of weeks en route back to the states after combat duty with the Marines on Okinawa. My brother-in-law, Lt. John Cull, a fellow Stanfordite, was Executive Officer of a destroyer escort that had been operating in the North Atlantic and was subsequently reassigned to Guam. A close friend and classmate in undergrad days as well as graduate school at Stanford, Frank Dowling, was stationed with the Navy on Guam. Passing through on a transport freighter and awaiting orders to return home was the ship's engineering officer, Lt. Art Wells. As mentioned previously, Art and I were best friends at Polytechnic High School and kept in touch in college even though Art went on to Cal while I attended Stanford.

The Marianas played a strategic part during the closing days of the war. The Air force used these islands to launch historic flights to Japan, dropping two atomic bombs. Japan surrendered shortly thereafter, and after "VJ" day, everyone's thoughts were centered on going home, but that did not happen right away.

The facilities had to be secured and supplies and equipment properly disposed of.

Personnel were contacted and offered to be returned home promptly if they agreed to continue to serve in the reserve. Most of us had all the Navy we wanted and just wished to go home. So we waited while the "reserve" personnel were shipped home first. As key officers left, their duties were reassigned to those remaining. Pretty soon, assignment after assignment was added to those of us remaining. I was given a number of unfamiliar duties assigned to me such as being responsible for the power plant, the food reefers and storage facilities, truck transportation, and heavy equipment facilities, among others. There was always a hope and a prayer that no disaster would occur while we were in charge of unfamiliar equipment, and ever one was looking for a lucky "rabbit's foot."

In addition to the long hours required to fulfill these many chores, we also had to use up the food supplies that had been stored for the anticipated invasion of Japan. No more fresh food use up what was in storage! Since the food was stored in large batches, we would go through an entire batch before we could switch to another batch containing different food. There was a long ordeal of some ten days when we had nothing but Vienna sausages until they were consumed and we could switch to something else. To this day I will not eat Vienna sausages!

But with the war over in the Pacific, the whole emphasis was on coming home and it demanded a lot of patience. On several occasions, there was news of someone who

Coming home on the MS Montrose

had been notified that he would be returning home that led to his deciding to celebrate. Unfortunately, drunken driving caused the deaths of several of these men who were ready to come home. A psychology developed among many of us to the extent that, after surviving the dangers of the war and with peace finally at hand, we were almost certain that something would happen to us before we could return home. This psychosis became so prevalent that some individuals were actually afraid to get out of bed for fear of something unfortunate happening. Finally, after twelve months service on Guam, I received my orders to return home.

On December 14, I embarked on the troop transport MS Montrose for a sixteen-day journey back to the states. Although everyone on the ship would have liked to have arrived in time for Christmas, they were all simply delighted just to be returning home. Christmas Eve and Christmas Day were very emotional experiences for all of us on board the ship. Returning Veterans of all ranks embraced one another and would sing Christmas carols. There was hardly a dry eye on board. Finally, on December 30, 1945, the MS Montrose docked at Port Hueneme in Southern California. As the passengers disembarked each and every one of us dropped to his knees and kissed the good earth of the USA. This was a most joyous, thankful, and unforgettable occasion, and we all gained an even greater appreciation for the wonderful country we call home.

While on board ship, passengers were allowed to send telegraph messages home informing families of our pending arrival; consequently, there on the dock, looking more beautiful than ever, was Barbara, waiting anxiously for her loving husband, George.

Chapter 5: USS Pittsburg Works

We celebrated the New Year of 1946 together in Los Angeles, then Barbara and I headed back to San Francisco where I was to be discharged from active duty with the USNR. I still had some six weeks of unused cumulative leave which had to be consumed before the discharge would be effective, so I spent part of this time shopping around for a job, even though my previous employment was assured under the "GI Bill of Rights." After considerable investigation, I decided that an offer from Columbia Steel, my prior employer, appeared to present the greatest opportunity and challenge.

Before returning to work for my employer though, Barbara and I used the balance of the leave to do some traveling first to Douglas, AZ to visit Barbara's parents, and then to drive from there to Laredo, TX. From there we proceeded south along the newly constructed International Highway to Mexico via Monterey, Mexico City, Taxco, Acapulco, and Vera Cruz. This was a great trip with many adventures. During the war, gas was in short supply and new tires were impossible to get; people "retreaded" their old tires to have something on their wheels. Mexico was most anxious to encourage tourist trade so they guaranteed that gas would be available. But tires and their repair became a task that required our patience and ingenuity and a crash coarse in speaking Mexican Spanish. The visit to Mexico proved to be a delightful and exciting adventure that we treasured for the rest of our lives.

In the spring of 1946, I accepted employment with Columbia Steel as General Foreman of an Electro-tinning operation that was to be installed in the new mill being built in Pittsburg, CA. This mill, utilizing the latest technology of "cold reduction," was a huge investment and the first such operation erected west of the Mississippi. At that time, our new facility was still in the design stages and was expected to be finished in early 1948. It was to be managed by a number of existing management people along with returning service veterans and new technical hires. All such personnel were to be sent for extensive training to other US Steel plants in the East and South where similar facilities were already in operation.

I received my training schedule, but was told that I would not be able to take my wife along because "this would be a very concentrated and time-consuming experience." This announcement became a crisis for me, and I pointed out that I had been separated from my wife for over eighteen months while in service overseas, and I would not put up with any further separation, even if it meant quitting my job. Fortunately, Joe White, the General Superintendent, was understanding and called me in, saying they did not want to lose me and would make arrangements so that Barbara could accompany me back east.

During the first part of 1946, the nation's steel mills were shut down because of a strike by the United Steel Workers Union. During March, a settlement was reached and our training program was put in effect. Barbara and I elected to drive to the east coast, stopping off in Douglas AZ. to visit Barbara's parents, then proceeding to Birmingham,

Alabama for initial training at the Fairfield Works of TCI, a US Steel subsidiary. By agreement, we could stay at the Tutwiler Hotel in Birmingham, where all the "bachelor" trainees were staying, for a maximum of two months until we found other accommodations.

In the "five points" section of Birmingham, we found a room to rent in an old southern mansion that was owned by Dr. Taylor, a female chiropractor. The house was old and quite run down, but most of the rooms were rented out. We were assigned a one-bedroom unit that had part of an adjacent small hall blocked off to form a kitchen, consisting of a two burner stove and a tiny green twenty-five pound ice box. There was no sink or running water in this "kitchen." Water was obtained from a small bathroom that we shared with another couple. But our unit, which was on the second floor, had a lovely screened porch overlooking a giant magnolia tree. Everyday, the iceman came and delivered twenty-five pounds of ice, which just lasted twenty-four hours during the hot summer months. This was home for about five months, and at least the two of us were together.

I went to the steel plant each day to learn about the new cold reduction process and to become familiar with all the facilities and processes required to make steel products by this method. The process started by using large hot-rolled coils of steel, which were unrolled and then "pickled" in acid, cold-rolled to the desired thickness, cleaned, annealed, temper rolled, side trimmed and processed by a Ferrostan Electro-tinning line (my assigned unit) into tinplate which was sold to can making plants. The experience was challenging but rewarding. Seminars and meetings were held often with the other Columbia Steel trainees who were in the area.

In September, I was sent to Pittsburgh, PA for a two-month visit to Irvin Works, another US Steel plant. The trainees all stayed at the grand old Schenley Hotel in Schenley Park and life was fun. We enjoyed the beer and great German food that was close at hand, and living on an expense account was pretty nice. With full lunches and eating out every night, it was not hard to put on weight. When I came home from overseas the previous December I was a scrawny 150 pounds, but in less than a year, I had ballooned up to about 190. That's what soft living does for one!

In October, I was sent to the steel plant at Gary, Indiana for another month of training, and then we headed for home. We found a duplex to rent in Pittsburg, CA which was new, convenient, and adequate. Another trainee, Joe Geiger and his wife, Lucille, rented the other unit of the duplex. Construction of the mill was underway, but a long ways from completion. Our main assignment was to follow the construction and to prepare training manuals that would be used by the crews to be selected once the facilities were completed

For recreation, I played rugby for the Olympic Club in San Francisco, and this provided me with a courtesy membership into the club and permitted me to use the gym and other facilities there. I was able to play during the winter seasons of 1947 and 1948, although the approaching mill startup in 1948 became ever time-consuming and brought my rugby involvement to an end.

During the fall of 1947, there was an organizational change at the steel plant that resulted in my reassignment from electro-tinning to becoming General Foreman of Cold Reduction. This was a big move since the cold reduction rolling mill was the heart of the entire new installation. Even though I had just been trained in electro-tinning I now had to learn a whole new process, and this meant returning east once again to observe operations at Irvin Work in Pittsburgh. Time was short prior to the startup so I had to absorb all this information quickly.

Five-Stand Cold Reduction Mill (Harried George Jedenoff, inset)

Bill Clark, who was originally trained for the general foreman job, was promoted to Superintendent of Cold Reduction and he assured me he would guide me along in the new position. Later experience indicated that this was a mixed blessing because Bill was extremely difficult to work with.

After two months at Irvin Works, I returned to California and started the process of selecting the key crew members for the new cold reduction mill. The plant's previous facilities, its old hot-rolled sheet and tin mill, employed some excellent workers. By considering people who had extensive experience in the old rolling process, we selected six individuals to become the Rollers and Assistant Rollers for each of the three shifts ultimately required to operate the new five-stand Cold Reduction mill.

In the fall of 1947, I escorted my three turn-foremen and the six key operators on a concentrated, two-month long, hands-on training experience to Gary, IN. We were assigned to Gary's operating crews and were coached by their experienced crew members. This turned out to be a stimulating experience, and we developed a friendship and shared a mutual admiration among the group. The last night of our visit was a memorable occasion. It was a Saturday night and the group congregated at Trainor's Bar in Gary, a place often frequented by our group. By state law, the bar had to be closed to the public at midnight, but the owners of the establishment asked our group to stay for a "private party" to be held in our honor. The owner brought out his own private stock of liquor and we all celebrated. One of the staff could play the piano so we all participated in singing and must have sung "California Here We Come" at least a dozen times. The party ended at daybreak but lasted forever in our memories.

Finally the big day arrived and we started "threading up" the new mill. All the plant executives were on hand to observe. Unfortunately, a vital, but unproven, part of the machinery the strip lubrication system would not operate properly. The critical sprays would just clog up. Without adequate strip lubrication it was not possible to get the necessary reduction. The Vice President of Engineering in charge had specified these particular sprays, in spite of objections from the operating personnel. Several modifications were made in the field which permitted the first coil to be rolled, but we were not able to get the required gauge (thickness), surface, or flatness. It was a complete fiasco. After several weeks of delay and major modifications to the mill, operations improved slowly on a "break-in" basis. The next few months were difficult and frustrating.

Long hours were expended by all supervisors sometimes involving 24 to 30 hours without leaving the job. We were plagued with equipment design problems, and with crew inexperience, and it demanded a lot of character to stay with the mission.

In the postwar period, the demand for consumer goods was very strong. and the mill could sell all the prime flat-rolled product it could produce. In order to fill our requirements, incoming hot-rolled feed stock (hot band coils) came from any US Steel plant which had surplus capacity. Most coils were received from the T.C.I. (Birmingham) and Gary Works. The latter, primarily supplied steel coils from an antiquated mill that was started up solely for our Pittsburg Works' benefit after having been shuttered for many years. This hot strip mill produced coils of marginal quality.

To make matters worse, incoming coils began to come in from a revamped rolling mill located at Geneva Steel in Provo, UT. The Geneva mill was built during World War II to produce steel plate and structural steel to support the defense ship building industry located in California and Oregon. The plant was built by the Federal Government (Defense Plant Corporation), operated by US Steel, and located in Utah so as to be far enough away from possible coastal attack by the Japanese forces.

After the war ended there was little demand for steel plate and the plant was shut down by the U.S. Government. Because of the adverse effect of the shutdown on Utah's economy, political pressure was placed on US Steel to buy the mill from the government and to continue to operate it. Subsequently, US Steel purchased the plant and invested considerable funds to convert the plate mill into a hot-rolled strip mill which could then provide hot band feed stock for the new facilities at Pittsburg, CA.

The conversion of the plate mill was a major and untried project. Plates had been rolled flat on a mill that was 132-inches wide. Hot rolled coils needed for cold reduction were generally in widths of 30 to 48 inches and in thicknesses considerably thinner than required for plates. Additional rolling stands and coilers were provided to permit the rolling and coiling of the thinner material, but the excessive width of the mill rolls created problems not previously experienced in the industry. Consequently, the Geneva plant had to experience a startup and development program of its own before it could roll product of acceptable quality. In the meantime, most of the marginal product was sent to Pittsburg, CA where every attempt was made to process it through the cold-reduction mill. During the subsequent period, there was a lot of finger pointing as to whose fault it was that the mill was not operating as expected. Because of our plant's inexperience, it was difficult to avoid blame.

Top corporate officials were unhappy with the disappointing startup and decided to bring in an experienced operating executive. In early 1949, Larry Dahl from Pittsburgh, PA headquarters was appointed Vice PresidentOperations, replacing our Lee Pringle who was moved to V.P. of Sales.

Top management elected to replace a number of middle-management personnel with some experienced "imports" from other US Steel plants. A dozen or so supervisors were transferred to the California plant. As a result, there was the general feeling among the local personnel that if one were retained on his job, it was tantamount to getting a promotion. With much frustration, perseverance, and great expenditure of time, the problems were gradually overcome, and the new facilities not only met expectations but eventually established production records as well. All in all, it was a great character-building experience, reserved only for the "young in heart."

As operations improved, individual performance was recognized. Fortunate "survivors" were promoted as vacancies occurred. In early 1952, I was promoted to Assistant Superintendent of the Sheet Finishing Department, where a new continuous coating (galvanizing) line was being started. In December of that year, I was moved back to Cold Reduction as Assistant Superintendent, and In July of 1955 I was appointed Superintendent. 1954 was a big year for the Jedenoff family a big promotion, privilege of a company car, construction of a new home, and the adoption of our son, Nicholas George.

In 1955, negotiations with the United Steel workers of America came to an impasse and the steel workers went on strike. Management employees were directed to stay in the plant to assure its safekeeping, and fortunately, there was minimal violence. I never forgave the union however because I was locked in the plant and missed my son's first birthday.

On November 1, 1955, I was appointed Assistant General Superintendent of the plant reporting again to my first boss, Don Rice. In early 1958, there were major organizational changes in the Columbia-Geneva Steel Division with our general superintendent, Mac McCall, being named Vice President of the Division, and my boss, Don Rice moving up to the General Manager position in the San Francisco office.

Red Morgan, an Annapolis graduate and a destroyer squadron commander in WWII, was promoted to General Superintendent of the Pittsburg Works, replacing Don Rice. Then on March 1, 1959, Red Morgan was promoted to General Superintendent of the Geneva plant in Utah, and I replaced him as General Superintendent of the Pittsburg, CA plant. With this promotion, it appeared that the Jedenoffs would stay put in that area for some time to come. Consequently, we elected to enlarge the house we had just recently built alongside of the Contra-Costa Golf Club, in order to provide more room for our expanding family, having just adopted a baby girl, Nina.

After the end of World War II, US Steel was gradually buying additional property in the vicinity of the Pittsburg, CA plant. Long range plans called for the ultimate installation of primary steel producing facilities at this location in order to convert the Pittsburg Works into a completely integrated steel plant. The location provided excellent access to ocean shipping for the necessary incoming raw materials, and for delivery of finished product to the various west coast ports. Engineering studies were in process to design the necessary facilities. This was an ongoing process with considerable manpower assigned to this project.

Meanwhile, Geneva Works was now the primary supplier of hot rolled feed-stock for the Pittsburg plant. Unfortunately, the quality of the product was still marginal and delivery performance was very unreliable because of serious labor problems at Geneva. Demand was strong and the local union at Geneva took advantage of the situation by staging numerous wildcat strikes in order to achieve their demands. Expedience ruled and management often yielded in order to avoid paralyzing shutdowns. Over a period of about ten years, Geneva workers participated in some seventy wildcat strikes and slowdowns, even though these activities were not permitted under the terms of the labor agreement. This terrible record was one of the worse of any major steel plant in the industry. Performance at the Pittsburg, CA plant was adversely affected by the unreliability of shipments and by the poor quality of the steel coils shipped. As General Superintendent of the Pittsburg plant, I complained vigorously to top management and provided detailed evidence to support my claims.

In late 1959 there was a major organizational change in US Steel. The President of the west coast Columbia-Geneva Steel Division, Les Worthington, was appointed President of US Steel Corporation. Mac McCall was named President of our division, Don Rice was promoted to V.P. and Red Morgan, who had been General Superintendent of Geneva Works, took Don's position as General Manager.

Shortly thereafter, I was called into Mac McCall's office and was informed that a solution to the Geneva problem had been decided. When I inquired as to how this would come about, Mac replied, "We're sending you to Geneva to straighten it out."

This is what happens when one complains too much! Consequently, I was transferred to the Geneva plant to be in charge of its operation with the rationale that my knowledge of Pittsburg's needs would help formulate the changes required at Geneva. Besides, acquiring the experience of managing basic steel operations would be invaluable in subsequently managing the completely integrated facilities that were being planned for the Pittsburg Works.

Chapter 6: USS Geneva Operations

Initially, my move to Utah was quite a shock for being transferred to the Geneva plant. For me, was like being sent to Siberia! The transfer would take place just as the major modification to my home on the golf course was being completed. However, as it turned out, the seven years spent in Utah were the most difficult, challenging, and yet rewarding of my entire career.

Shortly after New Year's Day of 1960, I reported for duty in Provo, Utah. True to form, about two weeks after I arrived at the Geneva Works, the union decided to pull a work stoppage in the Central Maintenance Department. This was kind of a "welcome greeting" and a subtle indication to me of "who was boss around there." I knew I had my work cut out for me. With help from the old hands at the plant, the stoppage was ended and the plant resumed its regular routine.

After arriving in Utah, it was prudent to keep my family in California until a suitable house could be found and until my self-organized training program was completed. Except for a very cursory exposure, I had little knowledge and no experience with the primary production units over which I now had full responsibility. Besides, I was an unknown outsider coming to a strange location. There was some natural concern about my selection. For example, the Assistant General Superintendent, Carl Forkum, felt he was more qualified and deserved the promotion. Fortunately, Carl was a very dedicated and loyal individual, and before long we became good friends and developed a great mutual respect for each other's abilities.

In order to overcome my lack of experience with basic steel operations and to gain familiarity with the plant, I elected to spend weekends in a learning capacity. Starting with Raw Material Handling and proceeding through Sinter Operations, Coke plant, Blast Furnaces, Open Hearth steel making, and the rest of the operations, I would devote a Saturday or a Sunday to each unit. I would select the general foreman of the unit involved and would place myself under his guidance as a learner and observer. I would be dressed in work clothes and was prepared for a hands-on experience.

At first this was a bit of a shock to the personnel involved, but once they accepted the sincerity and objectivity of my mission, things progressed well. It gave each foreman the opportunity to demonstrate his knowledge and also to discuss his problems. It was important that information so gathered was not misused and was not detrimental to the man's superiors. Mutual trust was vital and positive value was mutually obtained. The ensuing few months were educational and provided valuable knowledge, and they created some unusual friendships as well.

During this initial period a lot of analytical thought was given to Geneva's labor and performance problems and to what corrective action would be required to improve the situation. It would have been easy to place the entire blame on an irresponsible union. But what caused these problems to happen? The work force was made up largely of Mormons who were generally viewed as religious, industrious, and independent

Along one of the three blast furnaces at Geneva Works

people. How could they permit such a condition to exist?

In some areas of the plant there was a tense and uncooperative relationship between the front line foreman and the crews he supervised. Many of the supervisors were recruited during the war from other steel plants and were selected on the basis of their knowledge of particular operations rather than on their management skills. Many had little education and had worked their way up from the wage earner category. The people they now supervised were generally better educated, and thus in many cases, there was a "culture clash."

Most of the local workforce came from a rural and farming area, unfamiliar with industrial practices and obligations and with little concept of corporate economics. Some felt that the local resources belonged to the local people of Utah and that "foreign" Big Industry had come in and was making itself rich on resources that they had absconded. Sharp talking union leadership was able to convince many in the work force that there was nothing wrong in pressing their "rights" for all they could get from the powerful and wealthy Corporation. Even such activity as stealing company property was acceptable if you could get away with it. After all, it was just reclaiming something that was rightfully yours. Fortunately, many in the workforce did not share this view.

It appeared that to resolve Geneva's serious problems, it was necessary to get back to some basic considerations such as: improved supervision, objective leadership, improved communications, and an educational and motivational program designed to inspire the workforce to become more effective and competitive. Once progress was made in these areas, and as management improved its performance, a stronger position could be taken against improper union activity forcing union leaders to fulfill their responsibility to abide by the terms of the labor agreement. Irresponsible labor behavior would not be rewarded by appeasement, but would be handled with firm disciplinary action. However management must always ensure that it has done its own job correctly; only then can it be firm and can enforce company rules and regulations.

As General Superintendent, I immediately began a grass roots communication program, and this included my sending periodic letters to all employees and making daily phone messages that could be heard by employees throughout the plant, all with the intent of providing information of interest about plant activities, our competitive situation, new orders received, citing exceptional performances of individuals and crews, etc. The union initially labeled such information as "management propaganda," but the general reaction of the employees was favorable.

At the same time, an informational program was developed for front line management. A group of some twenty-five supervisors were taken off their jobs for four weeks and were scheduled through the various staff and service departments to receive a broader understanding of how their activities fit into the total picture of plant operations and what the plant, as a whole, expected from them.

Such classes continued until all supervisors had participated. The union labeled this effort as a "charm school," and claimed that it was an organized effort to "break the union." Oddly enough, about a year later, the same communication experience was provided to the various union representatives, with unbelievably successful results.

A series of informational meetings with all supervisory and management personnel was held with the General Superintendent and top staff heads provided specific information regarding plant performance. Charts and diagrams were used to show three aspects of plant operations: where we've been, where we are now, and where we want to go. Major emphasis was placed on the goals we must meet and what it takes to meet those goals. These meetings proved interesting and inspiring many of the supervisors had never seen the whole picture before nor had the opportunity of being a part of it.

Obviously, this was all a long-term effort and required time and patience. Special seminars in Labor Relations were conducted in certain trouble areas and where specific supervisors needed help. Basically, supervisors were told that they had to do their job correctly, abide by the contract, and provide good leadership then, and only then, could top management fully back them in case of a conflict. As supervisors improved in their performance, enforcement ceased to be a problem.

As organizational and communication progress proceeded, results in the operations of the plant became more favorable. It was time to take the next bold step: to obtain significant improvements in product quality, productivity, and customer service. A united effort, involving every employee at Geneva was mandatory toward reaching the goal of making our product superior to that of our vast competition, foreign and domestic. Getting full participation of our work force in eliminating "unnecessary work" and in "doing the job right the first time" required the dedicated desire to do so. It was time for everyone to share the responsibility and the rewards for the competitive success of our plant. Everyone had to be a contributing participant; we could not afford to have idle bystanders. Thus, through a series of grass roots meetings a united approach called "Errors Zero" was launched. In this effort every person was asked for his best effort and his ideas to contribute to our success, with proper recognition received for such efforts.

However, this cooperative team effort did not bode well with the local union leadership, which had held firm control over the workforce for so many years. They considered any steps to communicate directly with employees a threat to their local leadership and they labeled these steps as "union busting." The president of the local union was a former Welsh coal miner named Wilford A Biggs, who was reelected time and time again. His position as president was never challenged: in fact, the local union hall was even called the Wilford A Biggs Hall. In previous years he was successful in obtaining some ill-gotten benefits for some of his employees through the use of illegal pressure tactics. Many of the employees realized that these tactics were improper but just went along to obtain the benefits.

Labor's News and Views

Saturday, July 22, 1961　　　OREM, UTAH　　　SPECIAL EDITION　Vol. 1 No. 9

Union Officials Charge Jedenoff with Negligence & Industrial Immorality

We regard the contents of Mr. Jedenoff's recent letter in a serious light. The statements of Mr. Jedenoff are offensive, repugnant and represent Industrial immorality at its vilest.

Let Mr. Jedenoff know that he has not only failed and shirked his responsibility to maintain an operable mill, but that his conduct in trying to place the blame for his blindness upon innocent workmen is vile and reprehensible.

Mr. Jedenoff and Mr. Mazuria are both eminitely aware of the reasons why the mill will not produce. Break down after break down - All logged and camouflaged in record books. Break downs are current where repair is "Spit sticky" - "Enough to get by" - and it is accomplished without spare parts - without bolts or nuts. Directed by turn foremen and maintenance Supervisors who know that the repairs are inadequate and hap hazard.

We are deeply concerned about the condition of the facilities in the mill. We must earn our living with them - We are dependant on their efficiency. We deplore their present condition.

A few years ago the mill was a low cost producer within the Corporation and we were proud to be associated with it. Today, the mill is still a low cost producer, but we are no longer proud of what we see under the guiding hand of Mr. Jedenoff. Cranes are inopeable - soaking pit cranes still running full blast with the bottom dropped off - soaking pits burned through - pit covers falling apart and a general run down condition all over that is becoming the rule of things and not the exception.

A million dollar sheer was recently overhauled and then replaced with the same bad bearings because there were no spares. This is useless, costly and waste of precious, tightly alloted maintence hours. We realize this is an embarrasing situation to mention, but, by next month after Supervision has kicked this around, they will have convinced each other that the employees must take the blame.

BRAIN WASHING PROGRAM

We deeply regret that we are forced to deal with people that operate in the twi-light area and on rare occasions will act in good faith. At present a super brain washing program is being waged at Geneva by a past master with 20 years behind him. Mr. Jedenoff does not practive what he preaches. He repeatedly informs the Union that he will live up to the signed contract and then he refuses to arbitrate. The Company not only has the same right but the moral obligation to use the grievance procedure. Instead he makes his phonograph - telephone recordings regularly for the employees to hear and sends out letters to all employees full of half-truths and misleading statements. A deliberate attempt to pit one employee against another. One department against another and union members against their officers. He has been successful in some of his attempts to cloud the issues and try to create confusion and disloyalty among the rank and file people at Geneva. After the new furnace was on the line, the foremen repeatedly encouraged the men to file a grievanc so it would be a matter of the official record for the Company. Under the contract, the Union does not have the right to file a grievance for 30 days on incentives. Could it be that this top executive of U.S. Steel is asking the grievance committeemen to violate the contract?

The officers of Local 2701 have held meetings with the employees being charged with a slow down in the rolling mill area and they are trying to reach a sensible solution to the problem. The Union officers are convinced that the charge is a phony one and deliberately being fabricated and whipped into a frenzy by Mr. Jedenoff for the purpose of disolving the incentive program and at the same time operate the mill at an impossible speed with no regard for human life and no limit on the steel output. This sounds possible, but he proposes to do it with only a handful of men, a ton of bailing wire, and no down turns for repairs. He has been getting along somehow, but now he has used up most of the spare parts and he still demands increased production without any spares.

INCENTIVE PACE

The men are now working at an incentive pace. If they weren't, then why does the Company still pay them the high incentive earnings. The Company claims a 17 per cent impact on the incentive earnings and informed the men that if you increase production by 17 percent with no increase in incentive earnings, we will withdraw our charge of a slowdown. The men involved here reported that not even with an act of God could they increase production by 17 per cent. This 17 per cent impact deduucted from the indirect plans would leave about 2 per cent of nothing.

No. 4 On The LINE

When the Company built the new re - heat furnace, they stated that it was necessary to have more heat time on the slabs to cut down the slivers. This was the old familar cry. We want quality and this is the customer requirements, they say. Prior to the operation of the new furnace, the Company actually told each crew how much they could roll and would only permit so much on each turn through a system of controlled rolling. Now that the new furnace is in operation, we discover that the slabs were not too cold, but actually too hot and had **Continued on Following Page**

Continued on Following Page

An example of union resistance

Largely through the efforts of the communications program, employees began to realize that such tactics which resulted in work stoppages and unreliable deliveries to the customers, were harmful to the competitive position of the steel plant. As improved understanding and better team effort was developed, it is of interest that in a local union election some time later, two employees decided to run against Mr. Biggs for president of the local union. When the results were released, Mr. Biggs came out third in the balloting. The new president of the local was much more cooperative and with his help further progress was made at the steel plant.

In addition to better employee productivity many other steps had to be taken to improve the competitive position of the plant. Additional investment was required to modernize many of our facilities. In this regard an incident that occurred some two years after I came to Geneva is noteworthy.

Looking back, just prior to WWII, the Geneva steel plant was built by the United States Defense Plant Corporation to provide heavy steel products principally for the West Coast shipbuilding industry. Utah was selected partly because of the availability of basic raw materials, such as iron ore, coal, and limestone. The principal reason, however was that Utah was some 800 miles away from the Pacific Coast and therefore was not vulnerable to possible enemy attacks during the war. A young US Steel engineer named Art Weibel, was selected to design the plant's facilities. For the products intended at that time, it was a very good plant layout. As time went by, Mr. Weibel was promoted a number of times and ultimately to the position of Executive Vice President of Engineering and Facilities of US Steel. At the time of this particular incident, Mr. Weibel decided to visit the plant that he had designed many years previously. Geneva had many needs to make it more competitive for the products and the market it now served, and I took the opportunity to try to point these out to Mr. Weibel so that I could get his help in obtaining the necessary improvements. Mr. Weibel was a very brilliant, but cold, outspoken, and distant individual. As the visit continued, Mr. Weibel suddenly stopped and looked at me and said, "What are you worrying about this plant for? It's not going to be here two years from now." Of course this was not a very encouraging remark for a young General Superintendent who was working his tail off trying to make the plant more competitive! This incident also served as a personal challenge to prove Mr. Weibel wrong. History will show that the plant continued to operate profitably for the next twenty-five years.

In order to make the steel plant more competitive, many steps had to be taken in the areas of cost reduction, productivity, new product development, quality improvement, and market penetration. I established specific objectives for each of these areas. Regarding equipment modernization, we realized that we had to prove to our corporate management that we could produce our products profitably, and that their investment would yield a good return. In developing this program we made use of a "think tank" task force. We selected about a dozen management people whom we considered imaginative and knowledgeable. The members of this task force were relieved of their normal duties and were assigned to work full-time to come up with specific ideas of how to make the Geneva plant more competitive. Several excellent ideas were developed which were ultimately chosen for installation by top corporate management

Since the steel plant was located some 800 miles from our major markets, a strong effort was made to bring users of Geneva's steel products into Utah. Working with available state and local industrial groups, we organizing a new agency called the Utah Valley Industrial Development Association or UVIDA. This group was successful in getting several steel using plants to relocate to the state of Utah. Many other steps, too numerous to mention here were taken to build a stronger customer base closer to our steel plant, and Utah state officials were most helpful in this regard.

These various efforts paid off in a better competitive performance. After some four years, Geneva was able to work free from unauthorized work stoppages and achieved the distinction of being the safest medium-size steel plant in the nation as well as being one of the most profitable steel plants (in profit per tons shipped) within USS Steel.

In the spring of 1966, US Steel decided to hold its annual Board of Directors meeting in Salt Lake City. As part of their agenda the entire board visited the Geneva plant.

The board consisted mostly of executives from the eastern part of the United States, with the exception of David Packard, CEO of Hewlett-Packard Company of Palo Alto. The plane carrying our visitors arrived at the Provo Airport, just a short drive from the plant. On the drive we decided to give the Easterners a bit of local Western flavor.

Our friend, the County Commissioner Marion Hinckley, had a ranch on which he was raising buffalo, a rather aggressive herd, especially when aroused. As prearranged, when the bus came by the ranch, the buffalo herd came out roaring and snorting giving the directors quite a thrill!

During the plant visit, a slide presentation was made to the board showing "where we were; where we are; and where we expect to be." The presentation was very well received, and afterwards Dave Packard came up to me and exclaimed, "Great job, George. You really showed those Easterners that we "Indians" out West know how to run things!"

In early 1967, US Steel Corporation conducted a major reorganization. In May of that year, I was directed to meet with the Executive Vice President of Operations, Ed Speer, and he reported that he would like me to accept the position of General Superintendent of Gary Steelworks, the corporation's largest and most important steel plant. At first I was disappointed because I felt I was ready for the next step up, which would have been a general manager position, in charge of several steel plants. After all, I had already served as general superintendent of two plants, and I was approaching my fiftieth birthday. After considerable thought and consultation I accepted the position, and on July 5, on my fiftieth birthday, I boarded a plane in Salt Lake City and headed for Gary Indiana.

Reflections on Geneva

Looking back upon my almost seven years of service at Geneva, I feel that this time of my career was perhaps the most successful and important period of my many years of experience in the steel industry. It was a time when I matured and solidified the principles and convictions of my career. The experience I received at Geneva gave me confidence in my judgments and the opportunities to learn from mistakes as well as benefit from good decisions. At no other time in my career did I receive such an opportunity to witness the success of my own judgments, decisions, and actions. In spite of the scars and great challenges I had faced, this was the period when I felt that I became what I am.

This was also a very satisfying period for my family life because In spite of the heavy demands of my career, I still found time to enjoy my family and to see my two kids grow and develop. Our son, Nick, was in Utah from ages six to thirteen, and Nina was there from ages three to ten. During this formative time before they were to become teenagers they were a joy to be with. In the summer we had many family picnics in the beautiful canyons surrounding Provo and during the winter we skated on Lake Utah and skied at Alta and Park City in the Wasatch Mountains. Communicating with children is often difficult, but it is amazing what riding on a chair lift while ascending a beautiful wintry mountain can do to stimulate genuine communication. Perhaps it's the cold air and the exhilaration of anticipating the run down the hill that releases the vocal cords and permits meaningful conversation. As time went on, Nick became active with the Boy Scouts, and I had the opportunity to participate with him in many pleasant adventures. Nina took up dancing and became very proficient, and she also learned how to be a drum majorette. But skiing remained our most memorable activity.

The city of Provo had a special program each winter. On Saturday mornings, kids would gather at the Pioneer Park in Provo at seven, and a bus would take them to Park City where they received a ski lesson provided by BYU students along with the necessary lift tickets. I would take our kids to the park at seven and then drive to my office at the plant where I monitored the previous night's activities, read my mail, and caught up with my correspondence. At about 11:30, I would leave the plant and drive back to Park City to meet the kids as they completed their ski lessons. We would then ski together until the lifts closed at about five. This made for a delightful day for all of us.

In Utah I had become a big fish in a small pond. The Geneva steel plant was the largest and most important industrial complex in the whole state, and consequently it was not difficult to communicate with and receive attention from all the political and economic agencies in the state. As the Geneva plant resolved its pressing problems and became a successful venture, the prestige of being in charge of this operation became very flattering.

When it was time for me to leave Geneva for my transfer to Gary, an impressive farewell party was given in my honor. It was a distinct honor to have the Governor of the state of Utah, Cal Rampton, a Democrat, mind you, be present at the ceremony and to have him declare June 30, 1967, as the "George A Jedenoff Appreciation Day" in the State of Utah. Except for my subsequent service at Gary this type of recognition was difficult to emulate.

Gov. Cal Rampton of Utah, presenting me with his declaration

Chapter 7: USS Gary Operations

On my fiftieth birthday, July 5, 1967, I kissed my wife and kids goodbye at the Salt Lake City Airport and boarded a plane for Chicago. On the plane, in the first class section that I was entitled to use at that time, I ran into the son of the owner of one of our largest customers (EIMCO Corporation) in Salt Lake City. After he discovered that this was my birthday, he made sure that we had some red wine to celebrate. In those days, before jet aircraft, traveling by propeller planes was rather slow, so by the time we arrived at the Chicago Midway Airport, we had imbibed a considerable amount of celebratory wine. My assigned driver at Gary, whose name was Nobbie, was there to meet me at the airport. We arrived in Gary about midnight, and Nobbie dropped me off at the Gary Hotel, which I had selected to be my temporary residence until I found a house to buy, and then ultimately to move my family.

Aerial view of Gary steelworks

After checking into the hotel, I decided to take a walk to try to sober up a little bit. Although it was past midnight, the outdoor temperature was in the high nineties and the air was very humid. I kept walking and walking, but I felt no improvement so I returned to my room at about three in the morning. Little did I know how dangerous it was to walk around on the streets of Gary at that time of night, but good luck prevailed.

The following morning, even though I was still feeling somewhat woozy, I arrived at my new office, which was just a couple of blocks away from the Gary Hotel. I must admit that this was rather a rough start—a tough way to start a new job.

As a matter of interest, Gary steelworks was US Steel's largest and most prestigious plant. When he was chairman of US Steel, Judge Elbert H. Gary, had this plant built on the southern tip of Lake Michigan in 1906. Although Gary was by now an old plant, in recent years it had received major modifications to modernize the plant into a state of the art facility. Unfortunately, because of the difficulty in getting adequate financing, most of these new facilities were short-changed in the services required to make them operate as intended. This caused the steel plant to incur a lot of operating problems that greatly affected the bottom line. My two predecessors labored with these inadequacies but achieved little success. My immediate predecessor, Fred Dudderer, was promoted to General Manager and was the person to whom I now reported. This gave me the advantage of having a person who understood the difficulties involved, but it had the disadvantage of placing him in a defensive position concerning any radical changes that I intended to make. Fortunately, Fred was a very decent person and was easy to talk and work with.

Internally, my appointment as head of this major steel plant was looked on with considerable skepticism, because I was an outsider from the west and came from one of the smaller steel plants in the corporation. There were several executives who felt that they should have been given this promotion including two of the incumbent assistants at the plant who would now be reporting to me. One in particular, Charlie Kay, was pretty upset. He was a very knowledgeable metallurgist with extensive technical experience and was dedicated and hard-working and deeply involved in solving the technical problems associated with the new facilities. He was also a very feisty individual and thus had some difficulty working with people. As time developed, we managed to establish a good working relationship, although I doubt he ever fully accepted me as being his superior.

In addition to the facility problems which were huge, Gary had many other problems. Morale at the plant was low, largely because of several labor relations reversals, and the fear from some of the staff of not being backed up by their superiors. Thus there was a tendency on the part of many front line supervisors to be lax in enforcing rules and procedures. The union situation was a mess. Local union officers had been indicted for graft and irregularities, requiring the International Steelworkers Union to take control of local affairs. This was not a happy situation and resulted in lots of disruptive political activities on the part of the union. The city of Gary was constantly goading the steel plant to pay more taxes so that it could continue its fraudulent administration. It is noteworthy that in 1906 when the city of Gary was established, US Steel appointed the first mayor of Gary—a Republican. Since that time every elected Mayor was a Democrat, and the rumors were that every mayor became a millionaire after he took office! Three previous mayors had been convicted and were serving prison terms, but most of the other ex-mayors were too clever to be caught.

So this was the situation I walked into. There were challenges enough for a lifetime and then some! My first order of business was to get acquainted with the plant personnel and its extensive facilities. Gary works was a completely integrated steel plant, which consisted of everything from dock facilities for Great Lakes shipping and basic iron and steel making facilities to an extensive variety of finished steel producing units. The plant employed some 16,000 employees, and was the hub of manufacturing in the Midwest area.

During my first week I elected to tour all of the facilities in order to become acquainted with the supervisors in charge as well as with the plant. I started with the ore docks and other raw materials receiving facilities, and subsequently proceeded to the production units. By the end of the week I had covered all the units except for the extensive bar and structural finishing mills. On Friday afternoon I decided to visit these units in order to complete my orientation. Frankly, I didn't know at that time how extensive these facilities were. When I told my assistant that I wanted to visit these units he asked, " Which units do you want to see today?" I replied, "All of them". He just nodded his head and we started the visit. This was about two in the afternoon, but by six we had hardly visited half of the units. Not wanting to be embarrassed by my gross miscalculation I elected to keep on going. By nine in the evening we finally finished visiting the last of the mills.

I hadn't been on my new job for more than two weeks before a group of local union leaders decided to initiate a labor crisis in the central maintenance division. This problem had been brewing for some time, and the union probably thought this was an opportune moment with a new boss in charge, to take matters into their own hands. This disruption was quite a shock, but of all the crises which could have occurred, it was one I knew how to handle for the union at Geneva Works had trained me well. I took decisive action and immediately fired three of the ringleaders. My assistant, Charlie Kay, was greatly alarmed because he thought I should have checked with headquarters before taking such stringent action. In fact, Charlie roared into my office, and exclaimed "George, you should have checked with headquarters first. You're going to get your ass fired!" I looked at Charlie in the eye and retorted, "Charlie, if I get fired I will have the distinction of having had the shortest service of any general superintendent at this plant!"

My action precipitated a lot of frantic local activity. Because local union officers were no longer in charge, we had to deal with the International Union for a resolution. Discussions took place, but fortunately the plant continued to operate without any significant interruptions. Meanwhile, the grievance procedure for this particular problem proceeded at rather a slow pace.

About this time I had located a home to buy for my family in a community called Ogden Dunes. It was located six or seven miles east of the plant and was an attractive gated community. Our new home was located on Ski Hill Drive, a name that had obviously appealed to me. Since the labor problem appeared to be progressing normally through the grievance procedure, I felt I could leave so I flew back to Utah to pick up my family. The furniture movers were already on their way to Indiana and just as we were about to drive our car from Provo to Gary, I received a phone call telling me that the employees in the central maintenance division decided to bypass the grievance procedure and to bring the discharge problem to a head by proceeding with a full-scale slowdown. I had no choice but to leave immediately for Gary. Together with my family, we took the first available plane to Gary to be on hand for this latest crisis.

One of our plant guards flew out to our former home in Utah and drove our loaded-down car back to the new residence in Indiana.

After considerable discussion, planning, and preparation, I decided to take strict action regarding the labor problem. We took the unusual step of suspending the entire department of 280 employees. Meanwhile, necessary maintenance work was farmed out to several of the adjacent US Steel plants so that we could continue to operate without any shortage of services. In a few days and after many discussions with the International Union and after receiving their assurance that work would again be performed as necessary, the suspensions were lifted, but the employees affected were placed on probation. Work in the central maintenance division finally resumed to its normal level.

At the plant there was a large cafeteria where most management personnel, general foremen, and other staff ate their lunches. This gave me an opportunity to communicate directly with this large group of management people. Every day I gave them a status report of what was being done. Since the unauthorized action in the central maintenance division was a violation of our labor agreement, I knew that eventually we would win our case. The big risk of course was triggering a complete plant shutdown which would have been very costly to US Steel; however, I felt that it was extremely important to be in constant communication with our people in order to avoid such a calamity. The success of this action earned me some real "brownie points" with Gary supervisors. Luck was on my side again.

There were so many diverse experiences at Gary, that I feel I could write volumes about them, but I will confine myself to just a few of the highlights. When I arrived at Gary the incumbent mayor, who was an attorney named Martin Katz, was nearing the end of his term in office and had decided not to seek reelection. Since the city of Gary was about sixty per cent Afro–American and had had a long history of racial problems, Mayor Katz asked me if I would serve as a co-chairman of a committee called the Urban Coalition, whose purpose was to improve racial relations in Gary. The other cochairman was George Coker, an Afro American who proved to be a very outstanding individual and a pleasure to work with.

Not long after that, campaigning for the mayor's election began. Although Gary had never had a black mayor, the leading candidate on the Democratic ticket was a young thirty-four year old Afro-American lawyer named Dick Hatcher. Remember this was in 1968, so it was a most unusual situation for that time. If Hatcher were elected, he would become the first black mayor of any major city in the United States. The Republicans in Gary selected a white person named Joseph Radigan, a long-time civic-minded Gary citizen whose family had been in the furniture business for many years. Since Gary had never elected a Republican as mayor, it would be concluded that Radigan's election would be strictly for racial reasons. Tensions mounted high as the elections approached, and rumors had it that if Radigan were elected, the black residents would riot and tear the town apart. However, if Hatcher were elected, the white residents who were mostly of central European heritage would not accept a black mayor and would cause serious problems. It looked like a no-win situation. The steel plant, with its large black employment, would be caught in the middle, an innocent bystander to either consequence. Extensive special precautions were taken to avoid damage to the plant. As it turned out however, Dick Hatcher was elected mayor and the citizens of the city took this all in stride with no adverse reactions. Interestingly enough, when Hatcher campaigned for office, he promised his constituents that he would go after US Steel to force them "to pay their fair share of taxes," and then he would have enough funds to put "gold-plated doorknobs on every house in midtown." Statements such as these greatly infuriated top US Steel officials, and this caused problems for me later on.

Taking Mayor Dick Hatcher through the plant to inform him of Gary Steel's competitive challenges

Dick Hatcher's term in office did not start out smoothly. The previous administration, especially its white constituents, felt that they would all be replaced with Hatcher's backers. All kinds of municipal equipment suddenly disappeared. For example, various police cars were left with their batteries missing. Dick Hatcher had absolutely no administrative experience and he really had his hands full.

I realized that somehow we had to build a working relationship with the new administration, so I arranged a meeting with the new mayor. As expected, the meeting started out rather tensely with a strong sense of distrust on the part of the new mayor. I offered to be of service to him and to give any help that I could; after all, it was necessary for us to build as good a working relationship as was possible.

Dick Hatcher thanked me for my offer and said that he would appreciate another meeting in a week or so after he had more time to reflect on the situation At a subsequent meeting Hatcher told me that he had five principal concerns: (1) employment (Gary had some thirty per cent unemployment and many were considered to be "unemployable" and were referred to as "hard core"); (2) housing (mid town was overpopulated with occasionally six to eight people living in a single room); (3) education (a high dropout rate with little incentive to attend school);

(4) law and order (a decimated police department); and (5) administration (no experience in organizing his department).

I told him I could give him some help in each of these areas, and with the support and participation of a number of our very capable executives at the plant, we were able to give him significant assistance.

It was most important however, that our relationship was to be a "two-way street" and that the Mayor would be cognizant of the problems we ourselves were facing at the steel plant.

Hatcher had never visited our plant and had hardly any concept of what we were doing or of what kind of problems we were facing. He accepted my invitation to visit our facility, and after a half-day of observation he was pretty overwhelmed with what he saw. Hatcher was intelligent and obviously a quick learner. This meeting with the mayor was very helpful in bringing about a much better mutual understanding and working relationship.

The action we took to help Hatcher with his five principal concerns would be too lengthy to report here, but just as an illustration here are two of the areas that are of particular interest. In the matter of employment, Hatcher asked me to create some jobs for his unemployed people. I explained to him that we could not jeopardize our competitive position by creating jobs that we did not need. Although, at that time, there was a labor shortage in the whole region and we needed employees at the plant, most of those available in Gary did not have the educational or behavioral qualities to meet our employment requirements. However, we decided on a trial basis, to organize a limited and closely monitored program which would hire twenty of the so-called "hard-core unemployables". We worked with the Urban League in selecting them. George Coker, whom I mentioned previously, was a tremendous help in this activity. As a condition of employment each individual selected had to provide us with a "big brother" whom we could contact to ensure that this individual would appear on time, as scheduled, and would conduct himself properly. Also, each individual would be required to attend a basic educational session for one-hour each day on his own time. This was to continue throughout the probationary period (176 hours) allotted by our labor agreement.

We tried to extend this for a longer period of time but organized labor (USW) would not agree to do so. We carefully selected the supervisor to whom this group would report during the actual work assignment. To the amazement of many, this initial trial period went exceptionally well, and several participants in the program felt that this was the first break that they had ever received and were grateful for the opportunity.

The absentee rate was actually lower than the average for the plant as a whole. The educational sessions provided help in a variety of matters such as reading skills, basic arithmetic, and even such advice (suggested by George Coker) as to refrain from running out to buy a car and getting into debt now that they had secured a job. After this probation period, we started a second group of the "hard-core un-employables."

Several supervisors who needed people had requested employees developed through this program, but they were told that only those supervisors who had the sensitivity to work properly with these special employees could participate. This need provided an incentive for better supervision, and we continued this program, ultimately hiring about eighty employees whom we needed. Mayor Hatcher was very pleased with this progress in helping him achieve his employment objective.

The other objective of interest was housing. Since our nation at that time, had a Democratic administration under Pres. Lyndon Johnson, Gary (a Democratic stronghold) had received a number of financial commitments from the government to help solve its problems in midtown. Unfortunately, there was no place for the overcrowded people to be relocated to allow for selected midtown structures to be redeveloped as intended. This provided an unusual opportunity for mutual benefit. At that time, US Steel had a new subsidiary company, US Steel Homes, organized to promote housing made of steel, rather than wood or other common materials. There was a federal program that provided long-term loans, at minimal interest rates, to qualified non-profit agencies to enable building homes for low-income people. With help from Charlie LeCraw, a very imaginative guy who worked for American Bridge Company, we were able to participate in this program. A qualified sponsor was required to administer the project, and again we called upon our good friend, George Coker to have the Urban League accept the sponsorship. By working with US Steel Homes and with the Gary community, an appropriate site was selected and 256 units were approved for building.

We ran into some unexpected problems when we applied for the necessary building permits. Resistance came, of all places, from the residents who were located close to the site selected. These people were all Afro-Americans who owned their own homes and were concerned that a public agency near them would be a source of problems and would lower their property values. At this point I learned a valuable lesson; I discovered that there is no such thing as a singular "black community" as such. Within the black population there were as many strata and diversity of interests, backgrounds, and objectives, as there are in any so-called "white community." In order to get our project approved, it was necessary to convince the local group that this project would not affect them adversely and actually would enhance the attractiveness of that area. I received some valuable help from a very fine gentleman named Quentin Smith who was the President of the Gary City Council and was also a high school principal. Quentin was a big, strong, athletic looking Afro-American who was devoted to making Gary a better city.

Quentin and I conducted a number of community meetings to present the details of our project. Often I was the only white face at those meetings, but with Quentin at my side I had no concern. Eventually the local group approved our plans and we proceeded with the project. This turned out to be a very successful project, and it helped solve Gary's problem and it provided business for US Steel. Several months later, after I had left Gary and was located in Pittsburgh, George Romney, Secretary of HUD, came to Gary for the ground-breaking of this project.

Several other projects for the city of Gary required some financial investment and a proposal was submitted requesting these funds. When the proposal reached the desk of our Vice Chairman for Finance, Robert Tyson, he reportedly grew red in the face; slamming his desk, he screamed, "I will not give one single cent to that bandit who wants to put gold-plated doorknobs on all the homes in Gary." We had to find other ways to finance the projects involved.

Lest you get the idea that all these actions were strictly for altruistic reasons, let me point out that I felt it was extremely important for our steel plant to operate in a better environment. There was a shortage of labor in the entire Chicago area, and I felt it was paramount to have a desirable living area to attract and to retain good employees. In addition to the help that we gave to City Hall, I pursued many other civic activities that were oriented toward improving the community. Following a long Gary Steel tradition I served on the board of Mercy Hospital, the most important hospital in Gary. In the city and surrounding towns there were United Fund organizations, but they were generally underfunded and not well administered. One of my pet projects was to combine six or seven of these smaller charitable funds into a single, more efficient and viable organization. It took a lot of promotion to get the neighboring communities to accept this concept, because they all felt that once they lost their independence and became involved with Gary with all of its problems, all the funds would gravitated in the city's direction. By providing necessary ground rules and creating a proper administrative organization, we were finally able to establish a very successful North-West Indiana United Fund.

Meanwhile many operating problems at the steel mill still remained. A brand-new multi-million dollar facility developed by US Steel called the "continuous–continuous caster" was in startup status at the plant. This facility was at the cutting edge of new technology and much developmental work had to be initiated. The purpose of this facility was to be able to cast molten steel from many casts into a continuous solid bar, then cut it to size to serve as the feedstock for the finishing rolling mills. Prior to this time, a continuous caster could handle only one ladle of molten steel (approximately 250 tons) at a time and then had to proceed with the costly and time consuming process of getting ready for the next heat of steel. Gary's Caster was designed to process ladle after ladle of molten steel continuously without interruption. The concept was simple but getting there was another matter.

Because of the huge benefits to be obtained and the enormous costs involved in its development, this project had the attention of people at the top of the corporation. Someone from the president's office would call at least twice a day to get specifics on what was being done, what problems had developed, and why we were not doing any better. Thanks to the dedicated attention of my assistant, Charlie Kay, I had someone there who knew what was going on.

Several other major facilities, all underfunded, were also in a startup phase. This included a new giant blast furnace, and new steelmaking facilities. Such operations resulted in many very costly steps in bringing them around to expected levels of performance. Gary's monthly cost sheets were riddled in red ink. In our monthly cost reviews at headquarters in Pittsburgh, which I attended, the experience was never very pleasant. My predecessors at Gary had been subjected to the same continuing situation, not that this was of any real help.

It was obvious that productivity at the mill had to be improved. We needed more precise workmanship and a closer conformance with required rules and procedures. In order to help bring this about, I started a supervisors' training program similar to the successful one that we had established at Geneva works. Because of the large number of supervisors at this huge plant, we designed this program for just the general foreman level. About twenty such supervisors were selected for a two-week special training assignment. At the conclusion of each session, I met personally with each group for an informal question and answer session. Reaction to this program was overwhelmingly favorable as our supervision realized that we meant business and that we expected better performance. As a consequence, some improvement was beginning to be evident.

On April 4, 1968, about nine months after I had arrived in Gary, a national calamity occurred. That afternoon word was received that Martin Luther King Jr. had just been assassinated. Within half an hour there was a delegation of angry employees, mostly black, at my office, demanding that the American flag be immediately flown at half-staff or else. I do not respond very well to ultimatums! I spoke to the leaders of the group and explained to them that since the American flag was a federal symbol, I had to adhere to federal regulations in this regard. I told them I would contact the White House for proper instruction. Fortunately, very soon thereafter, President Lyndon Johnson directed all American flags to be at half-staff.

The entire nation was struck by this tragic event. In nearby Chicago there were riots and a lot of civil disobedience. Friday night at about dinner time, I received a phone call from the Mayor's office requesting my presence at an emergency meeting to be held in his office the following morning at eight o'clock. I arrived at the meeting as scheduled and observed that there were twelve to fourteen members of Hatcher's staff, all blacks, and there were just two whites – Bishop Grutka of the local Catholic diocese and me. Because of the seriousness of the situation everyone looked pretty grim. The purpose of the meeting was to try to establish conditions that would prevent any violence of the type being experienced in Chicago.

The mayor stated they hoped to have memorial services all over town, and he wanted some immediate recognition honoring the life of Rev. King. Since about twenty-five per cent of the Gary steel workers were black, and in a few areas such as the Coke plant and blast furnaces they constituted perhaps half of the employees, we had a manning problem. Most departments at the steel plant worked on a round-the-clock basis, and should such a large group wish to attend services at one time, we would have insufficient manpower to maintain the necessary operations safely. Obviously we had to find an adequate solution.

I suggested that we contact the various churches to see if we might be able to schedule memorial services around-the-clock so as to accommodate the demands of our workforce. The group accepted the suggestion but the mayor wanted to know how we would notify the citizenry. I said we would go on the radio and put notices in the newspapers. He laughed at that suggestion, saying that most residents didn't read newspapers or listen to the radio. I then suggested that we print notices and distribute these to the city residents, but Hatcher inquired who would pay for this and how would we get these distributed? In the group there was a big, tall, athletically built person named Lowry who managed the Midtown club for black youth. This gentleman was an active Boy Scout leader and was a recipient of the Silver Buffalo Award for his services. Incidentally he had the only air-conditioned building in midtown. He justified this luxury by saying that he couldn't engage with youth unless he could get them into his facility, and even if they came in, just to cool off, at the least this gave him the opportunity to work with them. He said that if someone would pay for the printing, his boys would deliver the pamphlets. I hastily volunteered to pay for the printing, and another crisis was resolved. Many other steps were taken at that meeting, and it is worthwhile noting that Gary escaped any violence as a consequence of this tragic incident.

An unusual event took place on January 15, 1969. Astronaut Frank Borman, Commander of the Apollo 8 mission and leader of the first team of astronauts to leave Earth's gravity and orbit the moon, was a native of Gary, having been born there. The town's citizens wanted to honor him for his historic accomplishment by organizing a "Borman Day" homecoming. Mayor Dick Hatcher appointed a Rev. Julius James and me as joint chairmen of the Borman Day committee. The primary public event was a Prayer Breakfast to be held at the Gary Hotel, and in order to arrange for this, Rev.

James and I had to drive to Chicago at 5:30 in the morning to pick up Mr. Borman and his wife Susan. We then drove back to the Gary Hotel for the function which was also attended by Gov. Whitcomb and his wife and many of the top dignitaries from Gary and the surrounding area. All of us present enjoyed the occasion with the possible exception of Frank Borman himself, who had trouble keeping his eyes open since this event was barely two weeks after Apollo 8 had returned to earth. My children, Nick and Nina, each received a personal autographed photo from Frank Borman as a keepsake.

As I look back on the many events that transpired while I was at Gary, a few of them especially stand out in my memory. There was, for instance, the big freeze one January when for the entire month the temperature never got warmer than 17°F. Even some water pipelines that were buried under five feet of earth froze and fractured.

Another event was when a severe windstorm with a peak velocity of 110 mph struck without warning and blew over a giant ore handling gantry crane which had weathered all the other major storms since it was erected in 1906. There was a freak accident in the rail rolling mill when a laborer fell into the path of the mill and was pulled through a set of rolls, and amazingly he lived to tell about it! In sad contrast, there was an unfortunate accident in the worker's changing room when a metal locker fell over and crushed to death one of our employees. Our city also experienced some traumatic events. There was the time when a racial riot nearly erupted in Gary when some blacks decided to rob an Orthodox priest at his parish. The priest was carrying no money, and angered by this, one of his assailants struck him with a baseball bat fracturing the priest's skull. Gary's original and older residents were primarily white Eastern Europeans, and they were totally incensed by what was viewed as primarily a racist act. Fortunately, speedy and effective action by several church members and black citizens, who were equally repelled by this despicable action, succeeded in preventing any violent reprisals.

In late January of 1969, US Steel Corporation announced a major realignment of management responsibilities in its production department. All of its steel plants had been organized into four major divisions, but now, after some consolidation, they were to be re-grouped into just three operational units: Sheet and Tin operations, Heavy Products operations, and Tubular operations. Each of these units would be headed by a VP with a General Manager reporting to the VP having direct responsibility for its plant operations.

Effective February 1, 1969, I was promoted to the position of General Manager, Heavy Products operations, with responsibility for eight steel plants. Although I had been in charge of Gary Steel for only nineteen months, apparently my bosses felt that I had done a reasonable job and that I had served my "apprenticeship." I certainly was not entirely satisfied with the performance of the Gary plant under my watch, but I felt I had made some improvements which would show results in future years. I reported to my new assignment on February 1. Barbara and the kids remained in Indiana to complete the school year and to find time to locate a suitable residence in the Pittsburgh area.

Looking back, my time spent at Gary was very educational, challenging, and significant to my progress. The job was most demanding and provided very little opportunity for anything other than professional activities. What little time I had for myself I tried to spend with my family. Because of my position in the community, I received memberships to two prestigious country clubs: the South Shore Club in Chicago and the Gary Country club. Unfortunately, I had no time available to make use of these memberships except for an occasional dinner and possibly two or three outings of golf during my entire time at Gary.

Our new home was in an attractive community called Ogden Dunes. Because it was a gated community, I felt that my family was safe there when I was not around. We became members of a beautiful little Presbyterian Church that was friendly and that filled our needs. The kids went to good schools and made friends in the community.

Nick became a member of the swimming team, and pursued his progress in the Boy Scout program which he had started in Utah. Nick succeeded in completing his requirements for the rank of Eagle Scout with his court of honor taking place after I had relocated to Pittsburgh.

Because we were located on the shores of Lake Michigan, we enjoyed precious time together on the lake. We bought a seventeen-foot runabout powerboat with a trihedral hull, which we named "At Last." Being a large lake, Lake Michigan was either perfectly calm or rough as the stormy ocean with the habit of changing from one condition to another in almost a moment's time. After researching the situation, we concluded that the only safe objects to navigate the lake would be either a cork or an ocean liner! Our little boat was like a cork and impossible to sink. It was a great vessel for waterskiing, and the kids became very proficient at that sport.

Chicago, with its many attractions, was only an hour away by public transit; consequently, Barbara was able to visit museums and enjoy stage performances in that great city. For all of us, living in Gary was another great experience of living in America.

Chapter 8: USS Pittsburgh Headquarters

On Saturday, February 1, 1969, I arrived in Pittsburgh and made arrangements to lease a unit in the Bigelow Apartments, which would be my home until such time as we purchased a house to relocate our family. The Bigelow apartments were adequate and located just three blocks from the "Big Ingot," which was officially the 525 William Penn Place building. This had been US Steel's headquarters since 1950, but apparently it had become too small for the growing headquarters staff. US Steel had purchased property about four blocks away and was constructing the new US Steel Tower at 600 Grant Street This new sixty-four story building was the tallest in Pittsburgh, and each story was approximately one acre in size. The building stood 841 feet high and was made of core-ten steel which had a coating of dark brown oxidation over the metal, preventing further rusting and requiring no additional protective coating. Because of its appearance the building was referred to as the "Rusty Ingot." When I arrived on the scene, the new building was just about completed and everyone was involved in making plans to relocate. This proved to be a major distraction and pre-occupied everyone, but the move to the Rusty Ingot was finally completed in late 1970.

U.S. Steel's new headquarters, commonly referred to as"the rusty ingot."

I reported for duty on Monday, February 3 and this was quite a traumatic experience. I felt like a country boy trying to navigate New York's Grand Central Station for the first time. Fortunately, while I was at Gary, I had established friendship with Jack Echel, who was the Administrative Assistant to the VP of Operations. Jack had been in headquarters for a number of years, and he really knew his way around. Jack was most helpful to me. How else would I know the location of the men's room, the rules regarding the dining room, rules and regulations regarding my expense account, arrangements to obtain transportation, and loads of other procedural activities with which I was confronted? Jack and I became close and lifelong friends and knowing him was one of the highlights of moving to the Rusty Ingot.

On February 1, US Steel's extensive production facilities were re-organized into the three aforementioned major units: Heavy products, Sheet and Tin, and Tubular products. My new boss was Van Leichliter whom I had never met before. Twelve years my senior, he had served most of his time in the American Steel and Wire Division which was located in Cleveland and had been president of that division since 1956. He was on the fast track to become president of US Steel as were several of his predecessors, but things did not turn out that way. He did not have his heart in his new assignment.

Before long, however, he and I developed a good working relationship, and he relied pretty much on my judgment and that made it much easier for me to perform my new duties. In general, however, things in the Rusty Ingot were pretty darn confusing, between adjusting to the new organization and being distracted with the move to the new headquarters, it became very difficult to operate "as usual".

Because of my change in title and increase in salary, my new position should be viewed as a promotion. But life in the Rusty Ingot was certainly different. As a general superintendent of a steel plant I knew exactly what my responsibilities were; there was a lot of prestige to that position. I had a car assigned to me and at Gary this included a full-time chauffeur. I had my own private washroom, and my air transportation was always in the first class section. In my new position, I was no longer entitled to a company car, I had to travel in economy, and I shared the men's room at the end of the hall along with everyone else on that floor. Even though I had the title of "general manager" I found myself at the bottom of the totem pole of the huge hierarchy of executives in the Rusty Ingot. I don't think I could've made it without help from my friend, Jack Echel.

As General Manager, Heavy Products Operations, I had direct responsibility for eight steel plants: Homestead Works, Clairton Coke works, and Johnstown works In Pennsylvania; South Chicago works, Waukegan works, and Juliet works in Illinois; Duluth Works in Minnesota; and Canton Roll and machine, in Ohio. Since I had never worked in any of these plants, my first order of business was to get acquainted with the facilities and the personnel of these facilities. I held monthly operating meetings with the general superintendents of these plants, usually at headquarters, and I would visit each of them once or twice each month to review operating performance, discuss safety issues and specific plant problems.

Since the general economy in the nation was depressed, our primary emphasis was on cost reduction and profit improvement. As would be expected, top management exerted a lot of pressure for improvement in these areas. The three operating divisions met monthly with the Administrative Vice President of Operations, Tom Hunter, to review performance. In addition, Tom was inclined to hold special meetings on at least a weekly basis. He was bright, very ambitious, but also egotistical and had an inclination to hog all the credit. He appeared never to trust anyone and had a habit of double-checking on any information given to him. This even occurred over trivial issues and always left one with a very insecure feeling. My friend Jack Eckel, who was Tom's Administrative Assistant, had very little respect for him and on a scale of zero to ten had him rated a weak zero! Tom had a great memory for detail and thrived on obtaining every minute detail in any investigation. I guess his claim to fame was that he remembered everything.

My buddy, Jack Eckel

Given the strength of our friendship, it might be relevant to describe how my relation with Jack Eckel had developed. I first met Jack when he was the Superintendent of Sheet Finishing at Gary sheet and tin mill while I was in training in 1948. I had only occasional contacts with him from that time until about 1964, when I was supervising the Error Zero program at Geneva. Jack Eckel, who had a strong interest in people and their performance, took special interest in what we were doing. Subsequently in 1967, when I was at Gary, a singular occasion brought us together. It seems that top management was concerned about the success of its college recruitment program, directed at hiring and retaining top-level engineering students. US Steel succeeded in hiring outstanding graduates, but many of them were leaving after only a couple of years of service. Exit interviews were held, but these provided only the negative aspects of their employment. The thought occurred, that knowledge of why some recruits chose to stay would be of more value. Jack Eckel, who was in headquarters at that time, came up with the idea of setting up a task force to discover some answers. A committee was established consisting of five plant general superintendents and a young representative from each of these plants. The young employees would be carefully selected: those who were employed for at least three or four years and who exhibited performance which appeared to indicate that they had high potential for future promotion.

I was selected to represent Gary works and submitted the name of an outstanding young engineer to serve on this committee. Because of my long-term interest in the development of future, high potential people, I quickly became a close working partner with Jack. We developed a means of obtaining valuable information from the young people who were selected to serve on the committee, and from this we were able to implement many improvements permitting people of high potential to find it worthwhile to continue their careers with US Steel.

This task force was still active when the February, 1969, corporate reorganization took place. Still serving on this committee, I had a better opportunity to implement some of the findings. For instance, one complaint concerned the lack of additional training or follow-up regarding the progress of young management personnel. We came up with an idea similar to the development program that I had established at Geneva. We decided to set up an extensive orientation program for management people within the corporation. A three-week program at headquarters would serve this purpose. Each plant was asked to submit the names of some of their outstanding people who appeared to have the qualities to rise within the organization. This group would include not only college graduates, but any employee, whether he had a college degree or not, who demonstrated the qualifications and indicated the performance that was needed.

With top management approval, this program was initiated and became locally referred to as the "charm school." Top executives from each of the staff and service departments participated as instructors, and I had the privilege of representing the production department in this program. A group of twenty-five employees from steel plants across the country were sent to Pittsburgh for a three-week period and were quartered at a local motel. For these three weeks, day and night, they were networking with corporate executives and among themselves. The overall reaction by the recruits was overwhelmingly positive. This made a lasting impression on those who were fortunate enough to be selected. Every three weeks a new group was begun and this continued for years.

It became evident that Jack and I shared much in common, and we really enjoyed our association. We both had a strong desire to circumvent the red tape inherited in a huge bureaucracy like US Steel and to find ways of getting things done. This was a monumental task because of the massive growth over time of the huge organization at headquarters. Unfortunately, in a bureaucracy there becomes a tendency for perpetuating staff members who can find fault with any suggestion and who find it comfortable and safe to delay or say "no." Because if you say "yes," you commit yourself, and if the idea doesn't work, then you'll be criticized for making a bad decision. Few people get fired for saying "no", but it's sure hard to get things done in an organization that has many negative decision makers. Jack and I had these guys pretty well identified.

Shortly after the reorganization, a serious problem occurred at our South Chicago works. Charlie Kay, who had been my assistant at Gary, was promoted to be the General Superintendent of South Works, which is one of the oldest steel plants in the Corporation. Blast furnaces require a great deal of cooling water that is re-circulated to conserve water usage. Several large settling ponds are used in the process to permit removal of any effluent materials absorbed by the circulating water. On one occasion, the earth dike containing the cooling water was breached, probably weakened by burrowing animals, and the cooling water escaped from the pond and poured directly into Lake Michigan. Before the dike could be restored, a considerable amount of polluted cooling water escaped into the lake.

The history of steel plants from an environmental viewpoint was not enviable by any means. Many years ago when steel plants were first erected, there was little consideration for dust and pollution being discharged. Since a great deal of cooling water is required in the process of producing steel, plants were always located near a good source of water, be it a lake or a river, and the processed water was discharged back into this primary source. Over the years a great number of technological steps were taken to remove and capture the effluents from the air and water. In recent years these environmental installations had become very extensive and very expensive. By the 1960s, the environmental performance of steel plants had shown substantial improvement; however, the general public was still not completely satisfied. Various environmental groups became quite proactive with sizable demands, many expectations unobtainable even with the latest technology. There was great pressure to install costly facilities even at the risk of financially bankrupting the organization.

The breakdown at South Works, even though relatively minor, made all the headlines. For several local environmental activists this appeared to be an opportune moment to further their efforts. Some felt that if such an incident could result in jail sentence of a top executive, this would serve as a strong message to the industry in general. Charlie Kay, who as General Superintendent was on his job for only a few months, was singled out in a landmark lawsuit against US Steel. Charlie was accused of being a criminal, and through his negligence he was branded "a murderer of innocent people." Charlie was one of the most conscientious people I had ever known, and these accusations were rough on him and his family for he took these charges very seriously.

The environmental activists were determined that he should be thrown in jail. Since I was Charlie's immediate superior, I had to do everything possible to support him and to prevent such severe action from occurring. It was extremely time-consuming for us to muster a defense. Our legal representatives demanded voluminous information, and Charlie was directly preoccupied in this process while still having to carry on all the responsibilities of running the steel plant. After months of preparation and litigation, the case was heard and US Steel was subjected to a huge fine. Fortunately, Charlie Kay was never required to serve jail sentence, but I don't believe he ever recovered from this galling experience.

Another serious situation developed at our Clairton Coke plant, which was one of the largest coke producing facilities in the world. This plant, located on the Monongahela River, produced all the coke required for the many US Steel plants in the Pittsburgh area. Traditionally, the volatile material in coal which is driven off during the coke making process is sent to an extensive distillation and refining process, known as a coke oven gas byproducts facility. In an effort to further improve the environmental aspects of this process, new technology was developed by US Steel to process and recover the valuable byproducts by means of a completely different process, using cryogenic technology and was referred to as the keystone process. Initially this process worked like a charm and was hailed as being on the cutting edge of technology.

Unfortunately after several months of operation it was discovered that the special stainless steel used in this facility was subject to degradation by some of the elements in the coke oven gas, resulting in serious corrosion and failure. This catastrophe was monumental in that all twenty coke batteries were tied to the Keystone process and could not be operated without the use of that facility.

The Executive Vice President of Engineering, Art Weibel, summoned top executives from research and operations to resolve this problem. In order to maintain coke operations, parallel routes were designed to bypass the failed units until such time as a permanent solution could be developed and installed. Every Saturday morning, our Executive VP of Engineering conducted a meeting at Clairton Works that I was required to attend. At great expense, temporary facilities were rapidly installed and the coke making operation continued. It was estimated that this disaster cost about a million dollars a day, and it took several months before the defective facility was redesigned and back in operation.

Meanwhile at Gary, the project to build the 250 housing units was making progress. Heath Larry, Vice Chairman of the Board of US Steel, called me to inform me that a groundbreaking ceremony involving this project was to take place shortly and that George Romney, who was Secretary of the Department of Housing and Urban Development, would be coming to Gary to dedicate this project, known as Oak Knoll Terrace.

Heath told me that he was unavailable that day and asked if I would take the US Steel company plane to Washington to pick up Secretary Romney and fly him out to Gary.

As mentioned earlier, on May 14, 1969 I had the pleasure of escorting Secretary Romney to Gary. I found Romney to be a very warm and impressive individual who was particularly pleased with the Gary project because he wanted similar projects initiated by private industry, to be developed throughout the rest of the nation. The groundbreaking dedication gave me a great sense of personal satisfaction and accomplishment.

Meanwhile on a national basis there was serious concern about America's competitive position. Foreign producers, especially in Japan, were making serious inroads into our markets. On September 17, 1970, Congressman Charles S Gubser, Chairman of the House Armed Forces Committee, called upon key government, defense industry, and commercial executives to assume a leadership role in upgrading the quality of products produced in America.

An advisory group of twenty-three representatives was called to meet on this subject.

US Steel's Vice Chairman of the Board, Heath Larry, was invited to attend but he recommended that I should represent the Corporation because of the program that I had initiated at Geneva works. I appeared before the committee and made my presentation, after which Vice Adm. Eli Reich, Deputy Assistant Secretary of Defense for Material exclaimed, "If I wanted a good description of what we've been trying to do in the manned flight program, it would be the one outlined by the gentleman from US Steel almost word for word." (see detailed coverage in the Testimonial section). Later, I received a letter from Dave Packard, who was Deputy Director of the Department of Defense at that time, complimenting me on my performance.

Shortly after this experience, I was invited by the US Army to make a presentation to their Senior Advanced Management Program at Fort Belvoir, Virginia. I spoke to a group of fifty-five officers all with the rank of colonel or above. The purpose of my presentation was to discuss management and leadership techniques in our industry so that they could compare methods used by the military commanders at a similar hierarchical level. On October 26, 1970 I appeared before the group to give my talk and then conduct an engaging question and answer session with the participants. This was a totally new experience for me, but it was helpful that I had been an officer during World War II, so I had some feel for the military. I appreciated outside opportunities like these, and it was a great experience for me, but I had the feeling that some of my superiors harbored some resentment because I had suddenly gained such recognition. That's the way things go sometimes.

The reorganization of February 1, 1969, proved to be short-lived, and the Production Department received yet another major restructuring on November 1, 1970. On that date all the steel producing facilities were realigned into just two operating divisions – Eastern steel operations and Western steel operations. You will recall that until that date, the production department consisted of three operational units: Heavy products, Sheet and Tin, and Tubular products. Bob McClure, formerly vice president of Sheet and Tin operations was named vice president Eastern steel operations, and I was appointed vice president Western steel operations. The other two previous vice presidents took retirement because of their age. After this reorganization, Eastern steel operations consisted of twelve steel plants located in Pennsylvania, Ohio, and northeastern USA. As VP of Western steel operations, I was in charge of eleven steel plants in the deep south, midwest, and far west. I had a general manager reporting to me whose name was Al Duff. This became a little awkward since Al Duff had been the general manager to whom I reported when I was general superintendent of the Geneva works. But as time went on we developed a good working relationship with each other. Al had a liquor problem, but after some serious discussions and an effort on his part, he was able to get this problem pretty much under control.

In our new responsibilities Al Duff and I were in charge of Gary Works, South (Chicago) Works, Gary-Elwood Tube Works, Duluth Works, Joliet and Waukegan in the midwest; Fairfield Works, and the newly constructed Texas Works (Houston) in the south; Geneva works, Pittsburg, CA works, and Torrance works in the west.

Jack Angle, Executive Vice President Production, in announcing these changes, claimed that, "This move would enhance management efficiency through geographical grouping of related operations and would by the same token enable a faster response to customer needs."

Al and I had a lot of territory to cover. We tried to visit each of the plants at least once a month and more often for the bigger operations. We usually could hitch a ride on the company plane for the Midwest and Southern plants, but would fly commercial to the far west plants. Once each month we held an operating meeting with the general superintendents of our plants to review cost and operating performances for the previous month. Most of these meetings were held at the Pittsburgh headquarters, but occasionally we would meet at one of the plants.

Bob McClure, the other operating vice president, and I reported directly to an administrative vice president, Tom Hunter, who was mentioned previously. My good friend, Jack Eckel, was his administrative assistant but had little respect for him. Still he was our boss and we had to make the most of it.

With the depressed general economy and with the effect of foreign competition, especially in the west, it was a struggle to get business and make a profit. The public outcry to improve the environment by reducing air and water pollution was having its effect. Demands for very costly, and often unproven technological facilities placed a tremendous burden on management at a time when profits were becoming more and more elusive. Plans for desirable facility improvements had to be postponed because of this pressure for mandated environmental projects.

On March 1, 1973, Ed Gott, Chairman of USS, retired and his position was filled by Ed Speer, who in turn was replaced as President, by Wib Walker, Executive Vice President of Accounting. This latter move was rather a surprise, but this appointment was undoubtedly influenced by the growing critical financial position of US Steel. Wib Walker had demonstrated good business know-how, even though he was only remotely familiar with the details of steel production and sales.

The traditional organization in most steel companies, including US Steel, was to keep the commercial and the production functions separate with their coming together only at the very top of the organization where the executive vice president for commercial and the executive vice president for production reported directly to the president of the company. As pressure was put on the sales and production units, each became more defensive and would turn to their superiors for backing. Consequently, problems that should have been resolved at a lower level sometimes crept up the line to become a "federal case." Lots of time was wasted spinning our wheels rather than resolving problems. These were not happy times at the Rusty Ingot.

Once again, US Steel's board and its top executives wondered if the current organization could be part of the problem. They decided that a study should be made to see if the organization could be changed to respond more quickly to the current problems.

A number of years prior, when US Steel consisted of a number of subsidiary companies, each subsidiary seemed to respond more efficiently to the marketplace. It was decided that a task force would be established to study our current centralized organization to see if it could be changed so that it would respond more effectively to our elusive customers. It was generally recognized that the west coast subsidiary, Columbia Geneva steel division, at one time, had one of the most effective organizations.

Ed Speer, while still President of US Steel, called me in and appointed me chairman of the task force. I assumed that I was selected because of my experience with the west coast subsidiary and because of my MBA education. Our charge was to come up with a proposed organization which would still be centralized but which would respond more effectively on a local basis. The task force consisted of several top operating, production planning, commercial, line sales, and organization planning personnel. Our meetings started out pretty much in a confrontational and militant manner since it reflected years of such behavior. Eventually, with considerable patience and positive thinking we came up with some meaningful ideas.

Our proposal was to organize domestic steel operations into four geographical units; each unit was to consist of both sales and production responsibilities and would be headed by an executive with the title of Vice President and General Manager. The four would report to a new position, Group VPSteel who would have the full responsibility of sales and production for steel. Pittsburgh headquarters would maintain a number of staff services that would be required to ensure that uniform policies and practices were maintained across the entire corporation. This was particularly necessary so that national customers did not play one division against another in order to negotiate a lower price.

Under this proposed organization each of the four VP's and GM's would have full responsibility for the profitability of their respective division. They would have to resolve any problems between sales and production on a regional, rather than on a national basis. Certain staff services however such as major engineering, research and development, facility planning, etc. would still to be centralized.

After considerable massaging and modification, a proposed organization was accepted. Heading this organization as Group Vice President Steel was Mike Curto, formerly VP of sales. The Eastern division was headed by Bob Smith (operations); Bill Haskell, formerly Exec VP–Engineering with extensive production experience was picked to head the Central division; Harron Bullard, a southern native and formerly head of the Alabama facilities was named head of the southern division; and Ralph Seely, formerly Western VP of sales, was picked as head of the Western Division.

Note that as chairman of the task force, it looked as if I had worked myself out of a job! However, when Bill Haskell vacated the Executive VP of Engineering position, Bob Ferguson was named to replace him. Bob had been President of a subsidiary company of USS, called USS Engineers and Consultants (or UEC, for short). Ed Speer called me into his office again and told me that in order to round out my experience he would like me to take over the position of President of USS Engineers and Consultants. Of interest, the November 12, 1973 issue of "Industry Week," in commenting about the reorganization, made this statement, "It's also thought that some of the assignments will give younger managers more visibility. For example, George A Jedenoff, one of those named by outsiders as a high potential manager, becomes president of USS Engineers and Consultants Inc."

It was also worth noting that one of the vice presidents who would be reporting to me in my new position was Fred Dudderer, who had previously been my boss when I took over the position of General Superintendent of Gary steelworks. As mentioned previously, Fred was a very decent guy and in spite of this awkward situation, we developed a good working relationship.

My assignment to UEC was not only a surprise, but turned out to be intriguing and provided me with new experiences such as negotiating and signing contracts with other companies and suppliers, and performing extensive travel worldwide. This latter activity proved to be very exhausting however.

On January 1, 1974, I took over the reins of USS Engineers and Consultants (UEC). Bob Ferguson, the new Executive VP of Engineering and my immediate superior was an excellent engineer but had a difficult personality. Because of some unpleasant past experiences, he had a bias against all operating people. This made our relationship a little awkward right from the start. My new company, UEC, had entered a contract with the government of South Korea to submit a proposal for building a completely new integrated steel mill in South Korea. Preliminary plans had been submitted and in late December, prior to my assuming my new position, I traveled with Bob Ferguson and several other UEC personnel to visit Korea and to discuss the preliminary proposal. This was an exciting experience, and we were hosted by the top people of Korea, including the Prime Minister. The new company was to be called TESSKO which stood for "The Second Steel Company of Korea". We spent a week in Korea meeting with the executives who were selected to manage the new company.

Korea was interested in our proposal but wanted USS to invest a sizable amount into the project; unfortunately, US Steel just didn't have the funds since we were under great pressure to make heavy investments in other projects, especially environmental facilities dictated by U.S. government mandates. Subsequent meetings were held with the Koreans at the US Steel headquarters where eventually we graciously bowed out of this project.

My new assignment involved some completely new responsibilities and areas of management. It offered an opportunity to learn and experience some completely different disciplines, such as negotiating and agreeing to major contracts involving clients not only nationwide, but throughout the world. It provided considerable opportunities to travel internationally and to learn more about the policies, industries, and cultures of other countries. On the other hand, it demanded considerable time away from my home and family and the travel experience was of considerable hardship and strain physically. As with all other new assignments, I approached these duties with optimism and enthusiasm with the desire to achieve positive results while gaining valuable personal experience. As president of this organization, it gave me the opportunity to exercise some executive and policy decisions even though the organization was small.

Still, my main concern was that I was shifted off to a lateral path away from the mainstream for promotion within the corporation. At that time the President of US Steel, Ed Speer, and I were of the same age so it was not likely that I would have the opportunity to replace him in the line of promotion. But there were still a number of top executive positions that were attractive to me, and my concerns about any future promotions were fed by intuition and a gut feeling. In contrast, however, I felt that perhaps my new assignment was a planned move to broaden my experience so that I would be better qualified for a higher capacity with US Steel. As mentioned previously, I approached my assignment with energy and vigor and lost no time in visiting clients in various countries. Even though I had the privilege of traveling first class or business class on most flights I had to learn how to sleep on an airplane and how to adjust for jet lag. I quickly discovered that new contracts were not easy to get, and it took a lot of time and effort to sell our services. It was a whole new "ball game" and fortunately it had its attractive and rewarding moments.

UEC had a number of projects worldwide that required personal visits. In order for us to accomplish these duties, we decided that we would split our activities by geographical locations. Fred Dudderer, my VP of operations, preferred Europe and North America. I concentrated on Eastern Europe where I could utilize my Russian language, and also the Far East.

We had a very important project with the Republic of China in Taiwan where we were building a complete integrated steel mill in Kaohsiung. Taiwan's main shipbuilding activity was located in this city, and we were designing a mill to provide heavy plates to service the shipbuilding industry. We also were hoping to market the US Steel designed continuous caster to this facility. During the eleven months that I served with UEC, I made five trips from Pittsburgh, PA to Taipei in Taiwan. These were quick trips and oddly enough I never had to change my watch because twelve noon in Pittsburgh was twelve midnight in Taipei. This was an exhaustive but successful enterprise.

I also made a few trips to Yugoslavia where we had several projects in that country. Here the younger people generally spoke some English, while the older executives were quite fluent in Russian so this helped me with my communications in Yugoslavia.

During my service with UEC I had many fascinating experiences—too many to discuss in this writing. During slightly less than one year I made trips to the following countries: Taiwan (5), Australia (1), South Korea (2), Great Britain (1), Italy (1), Yugoslavia (3), Japan (2), Venezuela (1), Austria (1), Germany (1), Spain (2), Brazil (2), and Canada (Québec Cartier Mining Company) (2). Needless to say, I got plenty of practice sleeping on airplanes and adjusting to jet lag.

While living in Pittsburgh I had the opportunity to attend meetings and serve on committees of the American Iron and Steel Institute (AISI), the principal steel industry organization in the U.S. On one such assignment, I became acquainted with a gentleman named William Roesch who had just been appointed chairman of Jones and Laughlin Steel Corporation. About that time, Mr. Roesch was contacted by the First Boston Bank to see if he would be willing to accept a position as Chief Executive Officer (CEO) of a West Coast company called Kaiser Industries. It seemed that the financial situation of that company was in trouble and a complete reorganization was needed. The First Boston Bank felt it was necessary to bring in an outsider in order to properly perform this reshuffling that was being supervised by Edgar Kaiser, the Chairman, and Gene Trefethen, the CEO.

Kaiser Industries was a loosely organized holding company that owned parts of publicly held Kaiser companies and subsidiaries. Bill Roesch accepted the position, but shortly after doing so, he had a policy disagreement with the President and CEO of Kaiser Steel Company, Jack Carlson. Jack had considerable service with Kaiser organizations, and he elected to take early retirement. Consequently, Bill Roesch was looking for a replacement.

Bill was aware of my concern about my future status with US Steel and asked me if I would be interested in becoming President of Kaiser Steel. He offered me more than double the salary that I was making at US Steel along with a number of attractive benefits. This appeared to be a great opportunity for me for it would satisfy my long term objective of ultimately becoming president of a steel company and because it offered an attractive salary. I gave this matter considerable thought and discussed it with a number of my close friends since it was a most difficult decision. Because I considered loyalty as one of my most treasured values, and I had been a very loyal member of US Steel for some thirty-five years. I just could not make this change without considerable tribulation and concern. Finally, I approached our Chairman, Ed Spear, and spoke to him about this opportunity. I knew better, but I had secretly hoped that he would give me some positive assurances as to my future with US Steel; however, he made no such commitment and at that point I decided to go ahead and accept the Kaiser offer.

Chapter 9: Kaiser Steel Corp.

In August, 1974 I traveled to Oakland, California to meet with Edgar Kaiser and other officials of Kaiser Industries. Kaiser's offer appeared to be a golden opportunity—one too good to turn down. On Sept. 30, 1974, I took early retirement from US Steel and on the next day, October 1, I assumed my new position as President and Chief Operating Officer of Kaiser Steel Company and also as Vice President of the holding company, Kaiser Industries. Thus at the age of fifty-seven, I turned the page and started a new chapter in my life.

Edgar Kaiser, Chairman of each of the separate Kaiser companies greeted me very cordially. As the first item of business he felt I should be introduced to all the important people in the community. Without losing any time, he scheduled a series of meetings with various political representatives, community leaders, and members of the press. The most impressive of these meetings was an elaborate affair presented at the Pacific Union Club, which included several hundred important people, including many of the top executives of our customers, and various companies with which Kaiser did business. This certainly got me off to a wonderful start with Kaiser's external organizations.

Internally I was introduced to Kaiser employees at a special meeting conducted by Mr. Kaiser. I knew that it would take a little time to convince Kaiser employees that I was a good choice and that It had been appropriate to bring in an outsider into the organization. Having had previous experience of coming in as an outsider, I knew that I had to proceed slowly and carefully. I spent as much time as possible circulating among the various offices at headquarters and getting acquainted with the people in a friendly and informal manner. I scheduled visits to the various Kaiser facilities to do the same thing. Initially, at least, this took off some of the frost.

Since Kaiser Industries was in the midst of reorganization, Bill Roesch brought in several new people to fill some of the key positions. In order to accommodate the incoming executives Kaiser leased a condominium complex located just a few blocks from the Kaiser building which we referred to as the "Kaiser BOQ," borrowing an old military term. I was assigned to one of these units which made the transition easier for it did not require my family to move immediately. Nina was still in high school and this permitted her to continue at the same school. Also this gave us more time to find suitable housing in the Bay Area and to put our home in Pittsburgh on the market.

With my condo being so close to headquarters I had more time to work on the transition to the new position. My relationship with my new boss, Bill Roesch, the CEO, was very good. He was very supportive and helpful, and since he came up through steel operations, we spoke the same language. Bill's primary attention was given to the reorganization of Kaiser Industries, so I was left pretty much on my own to conduct Kaiser Steel's business. As Chairman of the Board, Edgar Kaiser, conducted the meetings with the Directors of Kaiser Steel, but there was never any doubt that the person in charge was Bill Roesch. To assist him with the critical financial situation, Bill

Reviewing plans for modernization of the steel facilities at Fontana.(from left to right) Chairman Edgar Kaiser, CEO Bill Roesch, Pres. George Jedenoff

brought in a new Chief Financial Officer, George Forinski, who played an important part in all major financial decisions involving Kaiser Industries as well as the other companies that were part of Kaiser Industries

As President and Chief Operating officer (COO), of Kaiser Steel, I had a much broader responsibility than just the production and sales of the steel mill's products. I was in charge of iron ore operations at Eagle Mountain, CA, and coal mines and a coal preparation plant at Sunnyside, Utah and York Canyon at Raton, New Mexico. In addition to the main steel plant at Fontana, CA, Kaiser Steel had fabricating plants at Fontana, a Stamped Products plant (for automobile parts) at Montebello, CA, a mechanical and Structural tubing plant in Vernon, CA, and a large and versatile fabricating and large diameter transmission pipe facility at Napa, CA. The Napa facility used the Marine Assembly Yards in Oakland and Vallejo, and produced some very sophisticated assemblies such as giant oil drilling platforms that were used in the Gulf of Alaska and in the North Sea.

Kaiser Steel had full ownership of the United International Shipping Corporation and the Myers Drum Company. It also controlled Kaiser Resources Limited located in Canada, which was a major producer of coal for the Japanese steel industry and was principally owned by Kaiser Steel. Kaiser also had significant ownership in the iron ore facilities at Hamersley Mining Company in Australia. Bill Roesch and I served as directors of Hamersley, and we attended their board meetings every three months "down under." I also served on the board of Kaiser Resources, United International Shipping Corporation, and Kaiser Industries.

Each year the San Francisco Chronicle publishes a list of the best paid Bay Area executives. For 1975, Bill Roesch was listed as the highest-paid executive of a publicly held company in the Bay Area with annual compensation of $450,000. On the list of the top twenty, I was shown as number seventeen with a remuneration of $260,000. I couldn't resist pointing out that this was more than my friend and fellow Stanford alumnus, Jack Gray, President of Standard Oil of California (now Chevron Oil) was paid! He was listed as number nineteen at $247,500. It is of interest that forty years later, in 2015, the highest paid executive in this area earned 77.43 million dollars, and even number twenty was paid fifteen million. Furthermore, over 100 executives in the Bay Area received more than $1 million each that year. This as a good illustration of what inflation does over a period of years. During this same period, the Dow Jones industrial average went from 852 in 1975 to a close of 17,425 in 2015, a 20.4 times increase. Inflation has had a comparable effect on pensions, especially those based on a fixed income. What appeared to be an attractive pension in 1978 had had its purchasing power reduced some 75% by 2015.

With my greatly improved financial situation, I decided to indulge in some personal interests. In the want ad section of the newspaper I discovered a sailboat that was for sale at what appeared to be a reasonable price. It was a Morgan out-island thirty-six foot sloop. I had seen such a vessel in a boat show and was very impressed. The boat was located in a marina in Rio Vista not far from the Sacramento River, and after some negotiations I bought the boat. San Francisco Bay is a great place for sailboats. I kept this boat, which was named Flim Flam II, for over twenty years and enjoyed it thoroughly and finally sold it at a price comparable to the original cost. The other luxury item in which I indulged was buying a condo at Snowbird, Utah. The Wasatch Range, especially Alta and Snowbird are my favorites. As of this writing, I have been able to ski at these resorts every year since 1960!

In my reviewing my various Kaiser Steel activities, it was natural that because of my background I would concentrate first on steel mill operations. After making a close appraisal of the situation it was obvious to me that the productivity of the Fontana Steel mill was not what I thought it could and should be. After working with the Fontana people, I decided they needed some new leadership. I brought in my old assistant at Geneva works, Carl Forkum, to serve as Vice President of Operations. Carl was an excellent production man, and I knew he would be of great assistance. The cold reduction facilities were badly under utilized, so I brought in George Koss who had been my boss at Pittsburg Works when I was General Foreman of Cold Reduction. In the steel industry, George Koss was universally recognized as one of the most knowledgeable cold mill operators in the nation. To help me at the Oakland headquarters, I brought in two very capable people who had left US Steel and were working in other ventures. I selected Jim Will who proved his capability by later becoming president of Kaiser Steel and ultimately Chairman and CEO of Armco Steel Co, and Vince Noonan who worked with me at Pittsburg Works and was someone who knew how to get things done. The support from these two colleagues was invaluable.

The most pressing problems facing Fontana, however, were commitments to the Federal Environmental Protection Agency (EPA) and the CA State Air Resources Board (CARB) to make drastic environmental improvements at the steel plant. Although the nine open-hearth steelmaking furnaces were each equipped with air pollution precipitators, the removal of the effluent was inadequate; therefore, it was proposed that we install a giant topping precipitator through which the remaining gases from each of the nine precipitators would flow and then, presumably, the final residue would meet specifications. This was a costly and elaborate design that had never been tried before, and there was serious doubt if its performance would be adequate.

However its biggest disadvantage was that it would perpetuate the use of the open hearth process which was rapidly becoming obsolete. Steel making costs would be unfavorably affected without any improvement in productivity. Since the deadline for that commitment to environmental upgrades was rapidly approaching, I immediately ordered a review of our plans. It appeared to me that it would be more prudent to replace the whole open hearth facility with modern basic oxygen vessels which were more efficient, less costly to operate, and environmentally more attractive. The Board of Directors was informed of this possible change in plans, and they approved a feasibility study and approaching the EPA, requesting a time delay in fulfilling our commitment.

In order to proceed with the new plan we needed approval from the EPA, CARB, and the local environmental authority in the Fontana area. The EPA and the local authorities proved to be positive and supportive, but the meetings with the CARB proved to be most difficult. CARB chairman, Tom Quinn, had previously been Governor Jerry Brown's campaign manager. This was Jerry Brown's first term as governor and he rolled into office with strong liberal and union support. He brought in so many revolutionary ideas he was commonly referred to as "governor moonbeam." His Air Resources chairman had a very unfavorable opinion of big business for he felt all management was dishonest and could not be trusted. He proudly claimed that his agency had levied more than 1,100 separate citations at the Kaiser Fontana steel mill, and had levied more than one million dollars in fines. He reacted to our proposal as just another intentional stall in fulfilling our commitment, and he was determined to get everything he could out of Kaiser as soon as possible.

After extensive high-powered negotiations with the Brown administration in Sacramento, a six-month deferral was finally granted. Kaiser strongly objected saying that to design and finance a project of this magnitude would require a minimum of one year, but the state would not agree to such a time frame. Therefore we hurriedly put our engineering, operating, and financial heads together and proceeded to develop a plan which would replace the obsolete open hearths with modern basic oxygen steelmaking vessels. In order to achieve further economy, steel intended for sheet and tin products would be poured into a modern continuous caster and thus eliminate a number of steps required in the old process.

Apparently under pressure from the local steelworkers, the state required extensive additional work and increased crew sizes for the 315 oven coke battery. The final plan including extra demands by the state that ratcheted up the cost of the facilities to approximately $233 million. At this point Kaiser Steel had little choice but to approve the new plan. At that time, the economy was still quite strong and the improved facilities appeared to still be economically feasible.

With so many diverse activities all coming under the Kaiser Steel umbrella, there were enormous demands on my time and attention, but overall, I found these challenges to be demanding but stimulating. Edgar Kaiser had a number of strong relationships with several Japanese trading companies, and he scheduled trips to Japan to permit me to get acquainted. We were always treated royally. At this time, Kaiser Steel also participated in several industrial associations such as the American Iron and Steel Institute and the International Iron and steel Association. Bill Roesch was our official representative, but he always had me accompany him to these meetings. These sessions were generally very stimulating and informative, and they always took place in very plush surroundings.

An interesting situation occurred shortly after I went to work for Kaiser. A major breakdown occurred on the 132-inch hot strip rolling mill at Geneva that demanded at least a two-week shut down. This mill provided the hot rolled coils for the Pittsburg, CA works and such a major delay caused panic at that plant. Business in general was quite good, not robust, but good. Since we had some extra capacity on our hot strip mill, this looked like a great opportunity for Kaiser. Having a pretty good feel for the costs at the Geneva and Pittsburg plants, I came up with a price which would enable US Steel to make a small profit while making it quite profitable for Kaiser. Hank Huish, who reported to me at Geneva, was now at the US Steel San Francisco office.

I contacted him with a proposal to help the Pittsburg, CA works out by providing hot roll coils to that plant. Hank, who had been very concerned about the adverse effect on customer service if they were not able to ship out of the Pittsburg plant, was delighted with this proposal.

George A. Jederoff
President and Chief Operating Officer
Kaiser Steel Corporation

"Kaiser Steel is spending $233 million on a commitment to bring you more high-quality steel products and better service."

"Our primary commitment is always to you, our customer. Although we have employees and stockholders to be concerned about, too, it's in their best interest that we remain your most reliable source of steel here in the West.

"This hole in the ground in back of me is the site for our new basic oxygen steelmaking shop which will replace our open hearths by Spring, 1978. Our modernization program also includes a continuous slab caster to increase production of fine-grain and high-strength steels. Along with the increases achieved by last year's round-out program, we estimate our capabilities for finished product shipments to customers will be up by a full 15%.

"$233 million is a lot of money for us to spend on this commitment — it's more than we've made from our domestic operations in the past 25 years. And overall, we're planning to spend $100 million each year for the next six years on corporate-wide improvements.

"You see, we intend to become so valuable a supplier that you will be more successful because you buy from us. We intend to offer such a fine, high-quality product that we can expect the repeat business that comes from a satisfied customer. We intend to be price-competitive with foreign producers over the long pull — especially when you average out their premium price and lowest price years.

"That's our commitment. We're investing a lot of money behind it. And we hope it will earn us a commitment from you — to grant us a *preferential* position among your steel suppliers.

"By making sure we fill your needs better than anyone else in the Western steel business, we intend to build the kind of long-term relationship that's good for your business, *and* good for ours."

KAISER STEEL

You need us. We need you.

Kaiser Steel Corporation, 300 Lakeside Drive, Oakland, CA 94666. (415) 271-3211

For more information circle 14

One of many commercial ads designed to inform our customers of our approaching ability to be a more competitive supplier.

He approached his boss, Ralph Seely, who was in charge of the Western division. Ralph, being a salesman, always had some mistrust of operators, and he was concerned that I was trying to pull a fast one on him. Fortunately, Hank convinced him that this was a win-win proposition. Consequently, Kaiser received a huge order for hot rolled coils to fill the gap. The significant thing about this matter is that probably no one else but I could have consummated the deal. As it turned out, the Pittsburg Works was happy to receive our coils which were produced on a more modern mill and were larger and of better quality then what they had been receiving from the US Steel plant at Geneva, and this had a favorable affect on their productivity and costs. As it turned out, Kaiser made close to two million dollars on this order, so I felt that I made more money for Kaiser in that one transaction than what they would be paying me for my entire tenure with them!

After several months of concentrated activity involving my new job and living conveniently close at the Kaiser BOQ, I started to look at places where I could move my family. Fortunately, an old friend and business associate, Jack Putnam, whom I had met when he was peddling refractories for Kaiser Chemical, had since retired from Kaiser and was in the real estate business. He offered his services and proved to be invaluable. He searched the area and came up with a list of residences, and we narrowed down the list but did not make a final decision until Barbara had a chance to see these homes. Eventually we found the house on Wendy Lane that has been our happy residence for more than forty years. Moving back to California in early 1975 meant leaving my mother alone in Pittsburgh. We rented an attractive little apartment for her on Lake Merritt very close to the Kaiser headquarters where she could make some new friends and where I could come by regularly to visit with her. She stayed in this apartment until she became ill in 1976, and we had to place her in a nursing home in Walnut Creek. She passed away on Jan 31, 1977 at age 84, and was interned in the Serbian Orthodox cemetery in Colma.

After serving for a number of years, as a Director of the Association of Iron and Steel Engineers (AISE), the principal technical organization in our industry, I was elected National President for 1977. This required visiting various local chapters and presiding over the annual convention which was held in Cleveland that year. My duties were to promote the growth and the service it provided to its members and to assist the various technical committees and research activities. This was not only an honor but a great opportunity to become better acquainted with the various steel companies, their top executives, and the various companies which served the steel industry. In 1983, the AISE decided that there had to be better liaison with its local chapters, so it selected two former presidents of the AISE to serve as advisers to the executive committee and managing director. Richard M. Hurd, formerly of Bethlehem Steel and AISE president in 1976, and I were selected to serve the AISE on a part-time basis.

Our duties were to assist with program and district section activities, membership services and development, liaison with steel company executives, and work with long range planning and establishing goals. This was another enjoyable experience which I continued for several years.

I kept active with my volunteer service to Stanford, serving as Reunion Chairman of the thirty-fifth reunion of the Class of '40 and repeating as chairman for the next four reunions. I also served as chairman of all of my MBA Class of '42 reunions. In the spring of 1978, I, along with ex-secretary George Schultz and several others, was on a speakers panel for the Graduate School of Business Alumni Day. Later that day, I was one of three alumni who were honored for Distinguished Service by the Stanford Business School Alumni Association. I remained active in many service activities as well as fund raising for both the Stanford undergrad and GSB programs.

Meanwhile, the in-depth study of Kaiser Industries continued. and it became apparent that this company no longer served any effective purpose. It limited the growth of the Kaiser companies which it controlled. Since it was basically a holding company and did not produce anything separate from that of the participating companies, there was no good reason for it to exist. Furthermore, as an investment, it had the handicap of being a victim of double taxation. Since most of its income was derived from the dividends it received from the three public Kaiser companies that it controlled, namely: Kaiser Steel, Kaiser Aluminum and Chemical, and Kaiser Cement and Gypsum, the issuing companies were taxed before they paid their dividends, and these dividends were taxed again before they were paid out by Kaiser Industries.

The solution was for Kaiser Industries to go through a voluntary liquidation and distribute its shares of its three public Kaiser companies to the shareholders of Kaiser Industries stock. The wholly owned subsidiaries of Kaiser Industries, such as Kaiser Engineers, Kaiser Broadcasting, Kaiser Sand and Gravel, National Steel and Shipbuilding company, Kaiser Aerospace, etc. would be sold and the proceeds, after expenses, would be distributed as cash to the Kaiser Industries shareholders. Consequently, the three public companies would no longer be constrained by Kaiser Industries and would be in a better position to finance their own future needs. The first liquidating distribution to shareholders was made on June 3, 1977. With this program in effect and with the company of which he served as CEO (Kaiser Industries) about to disappear, Bill Roesch resigned on July 11, 1977 as President, Chief Executive Officer and as a liquidating trustee. Edgar Kaiser remained chairman of the surviving companies but not the Chief Executive Officer of any of them.

Although financially desirable, the liquidation of Kaiser Industries was an extremely emotional transformation for the Kaiser family, especially for Edgar Kaiser. The close ring of control by the Kaiser family no longer existed. Undoubtedly, he felt that he had failed to retain the traditional "home" for these companies that had been created by his illustrious father, Henry J Kaiser. The disappearance of Kaiser Industries as a company left many long time Kaiser executives and employees without a job. How was he going to take care of these people who had shown their loyalty to Kaiser for so many years?

In 1977, there was a flurry of activity involving the re-assignment of many employees. With Bill Roesch leaving Kaiser Steel as the CEO, Mr. Kaiser decided to replace him with a long time Kaiser executive. Edgar Kaiser called me in to discuss the situation in what presumably was to be a friendly meeting. He said he appreciated all that I had done for Kaiser Steel, but since I was there on a contract basis and that I had basically completed the plan for modernization of the Fontana plant, he decided he would like to terminate my contract. He assured me that I would receive all the benefits that had been promised to me, and as per agreement, I would continue to be on full salary for another year, so long as I would be available for consultation and did not accept full time employment with any other firm during this time. With Bill Roesch leaving, his position as CEO would be combined with mine as President and Chief Operating Officer (COO) and would be filled by a long time Kaiser employee. Mr. Kaiser selected Mark Anthony, who had previously reported to me as Executive Vice president, and whose lengthy experience was in the commercial and sales area.

I did not object since I felt that Edgar Kaiser had every right to make this decision as it would enable him to reward his old time loyal employees. Still, this was somewhat of a shock to me and I told him I had one serious concern. We were soon to embark on the startup of major new facilities at Fontana and traditionally, startups incur significant problems. Since Mark had no operating experience and I had "lived through" three previous major startups, I suggested that Kaiser retain me as President and COO until the new facilities were fully commissioned. During this interval, I would report to Mark as the CEO. Edgar thanked me for this suggestion and said he'd think about it and let me know. A few days later Edgar called me in and said that they preferred to stay with the original plan. Apparently Mark thought he could handle it without my help. I officially terminated my employment with Kaiser on October 31, 1977 and was on their payroll until November 1, 1978. Thus another chapter in my life came to an end.

Chapter 10: In Retirement

My experience with Kaiser proved to be rewarding; it gave me some new and interesting exposure. I received National recognition, I made many new friends and good business contacts, my financial portfolio was improved, I received membership in the prestigious Claremont Country Club, and I was able to return back to California which was my favorite area. Since I was being paid through most of 1978, I took time to reassess my future, to do some pleasure traveling, play some golf and spend more time with my dear wife, Barbara.

I always loved sailing and on November 1, 1978, Barbara and I flew to Saint Vincent Island in the Caribbean to join my ex boss and friend, Joe Clark and his wife, son and daughter to sail the Grenadines on a chartered yacht. This was a wonderful two-week adventure with just the six of us on board. Joe Clark had previously qualified to be able to sail the boat on his own without a professional skipper. An important feature of the Grenadines, also known as the Windward Islands, was that one always had a consistent wind and was never completely out of sight of an island. This was

Spending more happy time together

comforting in case a sudden storm were to appear a situation quite common in that part of the world. We visited about a dozen interesting islands which were pretty much out of the normal tourist traffic.

Meanwhile at Kaiser Steel, the modernization program continued with the first steel made from a new basic oxygen furnace on October 15, 1978 and the initial casting by the continuous caster on March 2, 1979.

The startup appeared to be going well and there was a great deal of premature optimism, to the point that Kaiser booked a number of marginal orders so as to get the benefit of greater volume. But unfortunately the usual start-up problems began to appear. Operations were severely affected, resulting in considerable down time and expense, and many customer promises to be missed. This was a serious blow to Kaiser's competitive position. Since the general economy had deteriorated and foreign imports were flooding the market, Kaiser's financial situation was severely affected.

The following year, 1980, Mark Anthony was relieved of his position, and he took early retirement. The magnitude of the problem appeared certainly more than what just one person could resolve. In desperation perhaps, during the next three years five different individuals served as President of Kaiser Steel. On February 20, 1981 Edgar Kaiser retired, and he was replaced by Stephen Girard as chairman, CEO, and Chairman of the executive committee. Girard was a long time Kaiser executive who had worked closely with Henry J. Kaiser and had direct responsibility for the former Kaiser-Fraser Automobile Company, and later the National Steel and Shipbuilding Company. Over the years, he served as kind of a trouble-shooter regarding many Kaiser interests. He had very little knowledge of steelmaking and his efforts to Improve Kaiser's Steel operations were not successful. With sizable fixed costs associated with its loan for the new facilities and its operations in red ink, the financial situation became desperate. Finally, in 1983, the decision was made to stop operations, and the steel mill was shut down. Furthermore it was decided to liquidate the plant and to sell off the producing equipment for the best price possible. Ultimately, in 1987, Kaiser Steel had to file for bankruptcy since its debts and obligations exceeded its assets and ability to pay off its obligations. It was a sad ending for such a fine company!

During 1978, while I was still being paid by Kaiser Steel, I explored the possibility of becoming a full-time consultant. Through my national contacts I became acquainted with two former steel executives, now retired, who were serving as full-time consultants. They both enjoyed their work and gave me some good advice as to how to proceed and how to protect myself from liability. My first client turned out to be Kaiser Engineers (KE), who needed some help in winning a contract. My friend and fellow Stanford alumnus, Jim McCloud, was President of Kaiser Engineers. I was able to successfully assist Kaiser Engineers and this opened the door for additional work with them.

The next year Kaiser Engineers provided me with an office and placed me on a retaining basis with additional per diem payments for work actually performed. This was a convenient relationship and was renewed annually for several years. I made many contacts for KE with various steel company executives and helped them to procure contracts.

One unusual assignment occurred In early 1983. KE had received a contract to study and propose an upgrade to an important steel mill in Skopje, Yugoslavia, called Rudnici I Zelezarnica, but referred to as RZS. As was common with most "Iron Curtain" countries, this company was partially "owned" by the work force and had a dual organization; one for operating the company in a conventional way and a parallel political (soviet) organization which supposedly served the interest of the employees. For example, the selection of managers for the primary organization had to be approved by the parallel soviet organization. Jim McCloud asked me to go to Skopje and research this organization and their plant operations for KE. This turned out to be a most intriguing assignment, and it lasted about four weeks. The RZS company had some very talented technical people and they were most friendly, hospitable, and anxious to learn. The head Soviet Official was a pretty sly individual who smiled a lot but avoided getting into details and proved to be an interesting case study. We were assigned interpreters who were women school teachers who spoke reasonably good English.They were bright and had memorized all the terms and names of all the equipment and facilities. I detected that this was all based on memory and that they did not possess a true knowledge of what they were talking about. I finally got one of the ladies aside and asked her point blank about her knowledge. She admitted not really knowing what the terms meant but was afraid to let her soviet leaders know. I asked her if she would like a quick course in steelmaking and she consented eagerly. I arranged for her and a dozen other interpreters to meet with me after quitting hours, and as we toured the plant, I explained to them what was going on. This lasted for a week or so and the women were most grateful for the experience. We became good friends, and they proved to be very helpful to the KE contingent which visited their facility.

My friend and former business associate, Ben Biaggini, President and CEO of the Southern Pacific Railroad Company (SP), called me one day with an unusual request. During the previous few months business was slow and Southern Pacific took drastic steps to reduce its workforce, including placing a number of their executives on early retirement. Suddenly there was a big pickup in business and they found that they could not provide enough serviceable locomotives to handle their needs. Maintenance had been neglected and the head of maintenance had been retired. Ben was well familiar with my background and asked if I'd be willing to help in making an important decision. He had an excellent engineer in his organization whom he was considering to put in charge of maintenance. This man, Bob Byrne, was technically very sound, but he had absolutely no experience in management. Ben asked me if I would work with him and decide whether or not he could handle the job. I told Ben that I would be pleased to work with Bob and that after a reasonable length of time, he could tell Ben whether or not he could handle the job. I told Ben that I could not coach and spy on him at the same time; I had to earn Bob's trust in order to help him acquire the skills needed. This turned out to be a challenging assignment, and since Bob was working his tail off, I was mindful of the limited time he had to spend with me.

Gradually we found time to communicate. One of my first objectives was to convince him that I was there to help him and that I was not interested in getting his job. He was a very intelligent person, and once he developed confidence in me we worked very well together. He was most anxious to learn and he learned quickly. SP had a number of shops where its locomotives and rolling stock were maintained with the principal shops located in Roseville, Sacramento, and Little Rock, Arkansas. I visited each of these places and helped Bob to improve their productivity by working directly with the shop managers. This was fulfilling work and quite satisfying since I was able to pass on some of my experience in getting more effective work out of a labor force.

Conditions began to improve and Bob was gaining confidence in himself. He often used me as a sounding board to try out ideas which might be unconventional and therefore subject to ridicule if they failed. One thing that I learned over the years is that whenever you chart out a new direction, be sure that you have a backup plan in case it doesn't work. The better the fallback plan, the greater the risk you can afford to take.

Ben Biaggini was pleased with the progress being made and asked me to work with a couple of other executives, including his Chief Engineer. He also invited me to attend a number of his executive meetings and asked me to participate in some of their profit improvement sessions. This was a real challenge considering the unyielding position of some of the departments particularly the Operating Division versus the Traffic (sales) Division. On one occasion, after failure to reach an agreement because of a stubborn loggerhead position on the part of the participants, a frustrated Ben Biaggini ordered his principal division heads to go to the Mark Hopkins Hotel and to stay there until a compromise position was reached. I was directed to attend with this group and to participate in the discussion which became very lively. I had nothing to lose and was able to achieve a resolution on an impartial basis. What an interesting study of human nature!

Ben continued to have confidence in me, and I continued to provide consulting services for several years. My principal contact was an interesting old-timer named Ed Ahern, whose title was Assistant to the Chairman, and whose duties were advising Ben on any number of issues including such items as merit raises for top executives. Ed was well past retirement age but he didn't want to retire and his know-how was of great value to Southern Pacific. At one time or another, Ed worked almost every job on the railroad, including track maintenance. brakeman, conductor, switchman, locomotive engineer, etc. He had a great memory and his experience was invaluable. And as the saying goes, "he knew where all of the bodies were buried." After overcoming his initial suspicion of me, we became great friends. When the State of California was planning the extensive Railroad Museum in Sacramento, Ed Ahern was assigned to the state as the principal advisor in developing this museum.

In the late 1970s and early 1980s my consulting business continued to grow. In addition to Kaiser Engineers, I performed consulting services for Bethlehem Steel, Bechtel International, Oregon Steel, ESI Wind Turbines, Judson Pacific Murphy, Envirotek, Ohio Rolls, Marawais Steel, and several others. It was always amazing to me that people would pay for advice from an outside source but probably ignore similar advice from in-house sources. Knowing that my retirement income was fixed and because of inflation would diminish in value over the years, I invested the maximum amount of my fees that were allowed by law into a Keogh retirement plan in order to partially offset the pending loss. This investment has become handy in recent years.

Judson Steel had installed some new facilities but they lacked the know-how to operate them properly. They needed some top leadership, and I suggested that they hire my old assistant, Carl Forkum, as VP of Operations. Carl had recently been released by Kaiser Steel in line with their desire to take care of their own long-term employees. This was a good break for Carl and he did a great job for Judson.

Marshal Wais, a wealthy entrepreneur and steel business associate, was interested in purchasing the idled galvanizing facilities built by Bethlehem Steel at Point Pinole near Richmond. He asked me to survey the facility and to advise him regarding the merits of its purchase. After receiving my favorable report, Marshal decided to buy the facility and I helped him to organize its operation. It was called Marawais Steel and needed an experienced person to start it up and operate it. I recommended my former associate and friend, Albert Sherman, Jr., who was nearing retirement age at US Steel in Pittsburgh and who was anxious to return to California. Marshall Wais knew Albert and offered him the job. Albert proved to be a very good fit and did a great job for Marshall, initially as VP of Operations and subsequently as Marshall's associate in a number of extensive interests that Marshall operated locally and in Europe, particularly in Luxembourg.

My son, Nick's college roommate and close friend, Wayne Bolio, had continued his education and earned a degree in law. After passing his bar examination, he was looking for work at a time when the economy was doing poorly. Wayne is a sharp and conscientious young man, and I was able to arrange an interview for him with the head of the Law Department at Southern Pacific who ultimately hired him. Being able to assist some of my old friends and associates made my consulting activity that much more of value to me.

This new chapter in my life proved to be busy, productive, and rewarding. I was pretty much able to set my own pace in taking on consulting assignments, traveling to many wonderful places with my wife, Barbara, sailing, playing golf, skiing, and doing volunteer work, especially for Stanford. Everything was going well until February of 1987 when it was discovered that I had rectal cancer that required major surgery resulting in a colostomy. Fortunately, the surgery was performed early enough so that the cancer was removed before it had an opportunity to spread. This was the good news.

The bad news was that I had to adjust to a completely new way of taking care my personal needs. Having been healthy all my life, this major operation that removed a vital part of my body was a complete shock to me, and It made for a very depressing situation. Furthermore, I developed some complications and had to return to the hospital for more surgery. In the process I lost some forty or so pounds. I was literally skin and bones and looking in the mirror was particularly depressing. After experiencing a period of depression and defeat, I took a good look in the mirror one day and was ashamed of what I saw a coward and a quitter!

At that point I decided, with God's help, that I was not going to let this situation defeat me. I was determined to regain my health and to go skiing again. Gradually I started an exercise and conditioning program to regain my weight and restore my strength. Thanks to gifts from some friends and after buying several exercise machines, I set up a little exercise facility in the basement of my house. I found that to maintain this specific program without interruption I had to ensure that I made a reliable habit of it. Without failure my routine was to get up in the morning, shave, and then begin my exercise program before breakfast and before getting distracted by other duties. By the time the next ski season arrived, I was ready and cautiously resumed skiing. I have maintained this discipline to this day! Daily demands to service my colostomy did not provide sufficient time and opportunity to continue my consulting work, so here again I turned the page and started another new chapter in my life.

Helped by literature from the United Ostomy Association and consulting with several specialized nurses, I was able to adjust my procedures so that I could resume a more normal life, including the ability to travel and attend events of my choosing. Ingenuity and a positive attitude can promote a flexible and normal life. As time went on, I resumed active participation in the AISE, Stanford volunteer service, Boy Scouts, and many other activities of interest. I played golf with the Claremont Country Club seniors, and I took advantage of our condo at Snowbird, skiing a week at a time, three or four times during the ski season.

In the 1980's, we purchased a condo at Northstar, near Lake Tahoe, and we used this condo summer and winter for it was a great place to bring the family and grandkids. But as the grandkids grew older, they had interests of their own and the condo was not used very much. In addition, the drive to our condo, in good weather, took about three and a half hours but at other times proved longer and more difficult, especially in winter. The crowning blow was when Northstar decided to change its composure from a family ski resort to a more extensive, multipurpose resort facility comparable to that of Vail, Colorado. This involved developing much of their property, building four story condominiums, boutique shops, restaurants, and hotels. Although this upgrade resulted in an increased value of the existing facilities, it completely changed the character of the resort. I put our condo on the market in 1992 and received an excellent offer that I immediately accepted.

Generally the period of approximately twenty years from the mid 1990's through the early 2010's was one of the most carefree and enjoyable times of my life. I still had responsibilities, many chores and activities but without the pressures that I experienced throughout my working career. I was able to do things I liked and spend more time with the love of my life, Barbara. We did a lot of traveling, mostly with the Stanford study-travel group, Vantage Travel, and on a number of cruise ships. We traveled on the Danube, the Rhine, the Volga, the Douro in Portugal, the Amazon (clear up to its source), the Po in Italy, the Seine and Rhone rivers in France, the Yangtze River in China, and the Mississippi. We traveled throughout the British Islands, along the coast of Norway clear up to the North Cape, throughout Europe, the Mediterranean Islands, the Greek Islands (Aegean Sea), North Africa, Asia, South America, New Zealand, the Caribbean, Canada, Iceland and Alaska. In Alaska, we flew to Prudhoe Bay at the extreme north to visit the oil rigs and the start of the famous Alaska (Alyeska) pipeline, then proceeded south along the pipeline (the only road available) to Fairbanks, visited Denali State Park and then traveled all the way to the other end of the 800 mile pipeline to Valdez where the oil is transferred to oil tankers. While at Valdez and Anchorage, we visited my college roommate, John Kelsey, who had been Mayor of Valdez at the time of the huge tsunami disaster of 1964.

Several trips to Russia enabled me to visit Balaklava, on the Black Sea, where my mother was born and the naval base at Crimea where my grandfather, Admiral Vasili Sipiagin, (my mom's father) had been stationed at that time. In Kiev, we located and visited the church where my parents were wed in 1910, and the Kiev Polytechnic Institute where my father received his degree as a mechanical (railroad) engineer.

Kiev Polytechnic Institute where my dad graduated in 1910

In Saint Petersburg we visited the famous Smolny Institute, which my mother attended. This institute was established by Catherine (The Great) in 1808 for selected girls of noble birth (Noble Maidens) and supported by the Empress of Russia.

In Kazan, along the Volga River, we were able to visit the general area where my father's family had extensive land holdings, and on our river trip from Moscow to St. Petersburg, we stopped to see Kostroma which was near the extensive landholdings which my mother's family maintained. We also sailed on Lake Onega and came within ten miles of my birthplace, Petrozavodsk. Unfortunately, I was not successful in convincing the captain to make an unscheduled stop in that city.

During this idyllic period I had lots of opportunity to participate in my favorite sport, skiing. Every year we traveled with the Stanford Ski Group. At first this was an official

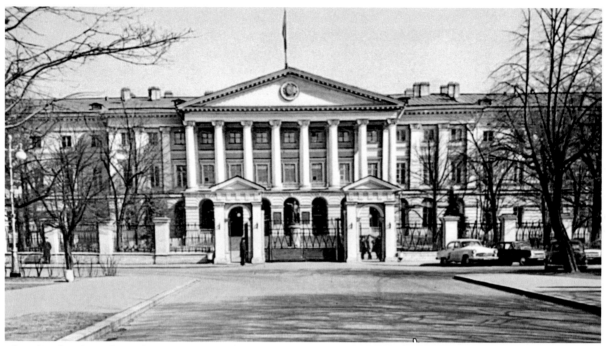

Smolny Institute for noble maidens in St. Petersburg, which my mother attended

Stanford activity, but later when it was no longer sanctioned by Stanford, the group, led by our great friends, Professor Channing Robertson and his lovely wife, Donna, continued to meet informally every year, skiing mostly at the prominent ski resorts in the Alps in Germany, Austria, Switzerland, France and Italy.

We also made a number of ski trips with the 70+ Ski club. This included summer skiing, which is winter skiing "down under," in Chile, Argentina, and New Zealand. In 1997, I celebrated my 80th birthday in New Zealand by helicopter skiing on the Arrowsmith Range near Christchurch. My good friends, the Quackenbush's, Bill and Ann Betts, Dr. Lester Hibbard, and "Mr H" (Harry Brandel) traveled with Barbara and me to celebrate this occasion.

This was the most celebrated birthday I have ever had. Starting with a birthday party organized by our daughter, Nina, before our trip, and concluding after we returned, I had a total of six birthday cakes to commemorate this occasion one of these on the mountain in New Zealand with the helicopter crew and guides!

More recently, in the winter of 2013, after I got home from skiing in Utah, I received a phone call from a representative of Ski Utah, the promotional agency for skiing in that state. They said they were embarking on a program to encourage more elderly participants to keep on skiing, and they wanted to interview me and perhaps make a video. They said that local TV station for ABC would also like to interview me. I told the caller that I was sorry but I was at home in California and through skiing for the season. He told me that Ski Utah would be happy to put me up in Salt Lake for a few days and to pay for my trip. How could I refuse such an attractive offer? I flew to Salt Lake and discovered that this experience was to have epic consequences. The two representatives who hosted me turned out to be two swell guys and have since become great friends. We met at Alta, and they made a video entitled "95 1/2 years young." This video was broadcast on YouTube and has had over 61,000 viewers – the most popular of any videos produced by Ski Utah. The TV station on network ABC had their own interview with me on the evening news.

Ski Utah was so pleased that it asked me to participate again the following year, which I did in 2014, again in 2015, again in 2016 and again in 2017. So far the five videos have garnered over 300,000 viewers on YouTube. On July 5, 2017, I became a centenarian and celebrated my big birthday skiing at Snowbird, UT. I had very extensive media coverage for Ski Utah made me a celebrity. All this is rather amazing since I'm not that great a skier; perhaps it means that you don't have to be especially good but just able to keep doing it longer than anyone else!

Another surprise to me was that anyone would be interested in an old timer in his nineties, let alone interested in giving recognition to a person like me whose accomplishments were performed many years earlier. Of course such recognition is flattering and a pleasant experience. The most important recognition was when I was awarded the Stanford Medal on April 18, 2009 for my many years of volunteer service to the university. Only three such medals are awarded each year, and this makes it a rare honor. In February, 2012, The Association of Iron and Steel Technology (AIST) published in its monthly magazine a two page article "AIST life member, George A Jedenoff." Marquis Who's Who publishing company which produces a number of "Who's Who" publications, included me for a number of years in the following volumes: Who's Who in America, Who's Who in Business and Finance, and Who's Who in the World. The Cardinal Society which includes all Stanford alumni who have lived at least sixty-five years since their graduation, has a luncheon every year during the reunion weekend. I feel honored to have been requested to serve as MC at this luncheon for the past five years.

In early 2010, Barbara had a physical exam after completing one of our trips, and our physician noted some memory loss and suggested a more detailed analysis. Subsequent examination revealed what appeared to be the onset of Alzheimer's disease.

Aricept, a drug used to retard the progression of this horrible illness was prescribed. Since that time, the effect of this disease, even though somewhat slowed, had taken its toll. I tried my best to take care of Barbara in our own home and did everything I could to facilitate her care, including installing an elevator since she could no longer navigate the stairs. I tried a therapeutic adjustable lounge chair, a hospital bed, a Hoyer lift, numerous grab bars, a transfer seat at the bathtub, and every gadget available. A reliable agency provided home caregivers, and I did all I could to keep her in our own home; however, her physical condition deteriorated to the point where she could no longer walk or even stand without assistance. The caregivers complained that they could no longer assure for her safety in our house, so I finally yielded to the urging of my family and placed her in a facility that handled only patients with dementia and Alzheimer's.

I was very pleased with the facility that was selected and also pleased with the excellent care that Barbara received. The site was ten miles from our house, and I drove twice a day (for lunch and dinner) to be with Barbara. I helped feed her since she was no longer able to feed herself, and I felt so fortunate that I was still able to drive so that I was able to visit her daily. We enjoyed seventy-five years of a very happy and loving marriage. We have been so fortunate and I felt rewarded every time I was with her, even as her mental and physical condition varied considerably from day to day. However, early in May of 2018, Barbara's condition took a turn for the worse, and she displayed some severe respiratory problems—unable to swallow, drink or eat anything. Finally on May 11 at 2:15 in the morning she passed away.

Barbara — Always bigger than life

This was a terrible loss but on the other hand it was a blessing that her suffering had come to an end and she was finally at peace. God in his infinite wisdom showed mercy.

As the final chapter of my life approaches, I want to acknowledge my gratitude to God for giving me such a long, productive, healthy, and happy life. I am so grateful for Barbara, and for the long and fulfilling life that we shared together, for wonderful children, grandchildren, and great grandchildren who have always been a central part of my life.

I am indebted to my parents for the sacrifices they made in getting our family out of Russia and for their strong influence and guidance as I was growing up. I am grateful for the wonderful friends that I have had some no longer living and some whom I have just recently acquired.

I love America, my adopted country, and also the long and satisfying relationship that I have enjoyed with Stanford University. During my life, not everything went smoothly. I made mistakes and some bad decisions, occasionally exercising some poor judgment, but, overall, I am pleased with what I have accomplished. Most of my ambitions and goals have been attained. Not all, of course, but what can you expect from a perennial optimist?

Now that I have begun my second century of life, I appreciate this opportunity to look back on 100 years of experiences and to share these with others.

SECTION TWO
My Family

Chapter 11: My Dad and Jedenoff Family

Alexander Nikolaevich Jedenoff (my father) was born on June 22, 1885 in Penza and was registered on November 1, 1901 by his father in the sixth part of the book of Russian Nobility, Pensenskoi Gubernia. He attended the Real School in Penza, graduating in 1903. Then he was accepted in Kiev Polytechnic Institute, Russia's premier technical college, where he graduated as a mechanical engineer in 1911.

Alexander Nikolaevich Jedenoff, my father

He began a career in railroading, qualifying as a "Revisor Dvazhenia" (literally translated as "Inspector of Operations"). His service with the Russian Railway System involved being located in a number of cities: Moscow, Perm, Akhtubinsk, Taganrog, Samara, and Petrozavodsk. His last position in Russia was Assistant Traffic Manager of the Perm Railroad.

Alexander Nikolaevich married Barbara Vasilievna Sipiagina, daughter of a noble family, on January 23, 1910 in Kiev. They had two sons: Alexai Alexandrovich, born on March 25, 1911 in Taganrog (along the Sea of Azov), and Georgi Alexandrovich, born on July 5, 1917, in Petrozavodsk, Russia.

As described earlier, once the Bolshevik revolution started in St. Petersburg in November of 1917, it became necessary to move out of that troubled area. In order to safeguard his family, my father was transferred to various cities considered to be safer, and subsequently to Harbin, Manchuria

Finally, the family emigrated to the United States, arriving in Seattle, WA. on March 3, 1923. My father continued to live in Seattle and was employed by the Great Northern Northern Pacific Railroads (King Street Station). Adjusting to life and work in a new country was most difficult because of the different language and culture, and though he was a highly-trained engineer he was never able to advance beyond serving as a mechanical inspector at the station. He retired in 1959, after thirty-six years of service.

My father was president of the Seattle Chapter of the Russian World War Veterans; a member of the Noble Society of Russian Descent; the Russian Orphan Children's Society, and the Saint Spiridon's Russian Orthodox Cathedral parish. He received the Order of the Compassionate Heart from the Russian Veterans Society of the World War, for his service to Russian Disabled Veterans of World War I, and the Order of St Nicholas for service to the Russian community.

Throughout his life in America he was an active member of the Republican Party and devoted considerable effort to communicating to public groups about the dangers and pitfalls of the Communist movement in the United States. He passed away on January 29,1962, in Seattle, Washington.

My Dad's father (my grandfather), Nikolai Nikolaevich II, was born on his father's estate in Sanderki and was registered in the book of Pensenskoi Gubernia. He attended a Gymnasium for Nobility in Penza. In his youth he participated in the revolutionary (populist) movement and in 1881 was expelled for a year from Moscow University for participating in student riots. He enrolled in University of Kazan and graduated as a lawyer. He held the position of Zemsky Nachalnick ("Chief of Land-holdings"), and he inherited his father's estate in Sanderki where he chose to live. He was elected a member of the Zemsky Uprava. Apparently, he died in 1934 in Rostofnadonu.

He had a brother, Georgi Nikolaevich, a titular counselor and also a military

Nikolai Nikolaevich II, my grandfather

surgeon. Nikolai Nikolaevich II had five children: Michael (who was lost in a naval battle near Vladivostok on the ship "Magnet"), Sviatoslav, Alexander (my father), Natasha, and Olga.

The history of the family of Jedenoffs has been traced back to the time of Czar Ivan the-Terrible (Ivan IV, 1547-1584), and the Jedenoff family crest was established during that time.

65

Герб рода

1 Стр.

Жеденовыхъ.

Въ голубомъ полѣ щита изображены двѣ крестообразно положенныя шпаги, остроконечіями вверхъ и посрединѣ оныхъ золотый ключъ. Щитъ увѣнчанъ дворянскимъ шлемомъ и короною съ тремя на оной строусовыми перьями. Наметъ на щитѣ голубый, подложенный серебромъ.

The Jedenoff family crest

Chapter 12: My Mother and the Sipiagins

My mother, Varvara (Barbara) Vacilievna, was born on October 27, 1892 (some references state 1888) in Balaklava, Crimea while her father was serving with the Russian Navy in Sevastopol at the Russian Imperial Naval Base on the Black Sea.

Barbara was the youngest in the family and had one sister, Tatiana (who married Admiral Nikolae Nikanov), and three brothers: Iakov (Yasha) (born January 19,1883) , John (Vania) (born May 5,1885), and Illia (born July 9,1886).

Two of her brothers, Yasha and Vania were officers in the Czar's Navy, while Illia served with the Naval Ministry in a civilian capacity. It was reported that Vania was executed by the Bolsheviks, while the fate of the others is not known.

Barbara Vacilievna Jedenoff, 1928

Barbara's Siblings: Tatiana, Vasha, Vania and Illia

Barbara Jedenoff grew up on her family's estate at Oranienbaum, near St. Petersburg on the Gulf of Finland. She was a graduate of the Smolny Institute in St. Petersburg, established by Catherine-the-Great for girls of the nobility. She was an accomplished pianist and played in concerts for the Empress Alexandra.

She married Alexander Nikolaevich Jedenoff on January 23, 1910 in Kiev. They had two sons: Alexae (Alexis) Alexandrovich and Georgi (George) Alexandrovich.

As a consequence of the Russian revolution, the Jedenoff family immigrated to America, arriving in Seattle, WA. in 1923. The economic situation was very difficult, especially for recent immigrants who spoke no English.

While raising her two sons, my mother gave piano lessons to supplement the family income.

Family tensions became unbearable, so she and my father separated and were subsequently divorced in 1930. She was awarded custody of her younger son, George, and the two of them moved to the San Francisco Bay area in 1932.

She remarried in 1934 to a former Russian Czarist Officer, Georgi Ivanovich Shishko, recipient of the St. George Cross for military gallantry, the highest award granted by the Czar.

During the depression, jobs became very scarce. Mr. Shishko worked in construction labor, building the water system for the City of San Francisco (Hetch Hetchy& Mokelumne Project), until that project was completed. There was a long period of unemployment as jobs just were not available. Finally he gained employment with the City of San Francisco at the airport.

Vacili Nikolaevich Sipiagin, my grandfather

Life was still difficult and Barbara divorced again in 1964. She continued to live in San Francisco until moving to Pittsburgh, PA in 1972 to be with her son, George. She moved back to Oakland in 1974 when he accepted employment with Kaiser Steel.

Barbara was able to stay in touch with her sister, Tatiana, who escaped to France from the Russian Revolution. Her husband, Admiral Nicholai Nikanov, was able to join her and they lived the rest of their lives in France.

My mother, Barbara V. Jedenoff, died on January 31, 1977 in Walnut Creek, CA at age 88.

Barbara's father was Vacili Nikolaevich Sipiagin who served in the Turkish War and became a confident of Czar Nicholas II. He served as staff-captain, then Right State Councilor (in civil service). He was born 16 March, 1855. In 1887 he was assigned to the Navy, as Staff Officer (civil rank) in the Port of Kronstadt and in 1889 was appointed Overseer of Sevastopil Naval Hospital.

In 1907 he headed the Archives of the Ministry of the Navy (later renamed the Russian State Naval Archives).

He was promoted to Privy Councilor (which corresponds to Lt. General or Vice Admiral), and then he retired for reasons of health. Upon retirement, he lived with his family in the province of Liflandia (now a part of Latvia and Estonia). It is my understanding that during the revolution he was arrested by the Bolsheviks and confined to a prison where he died.

In the Russian Biographical Slovar (Encyclopedia), dated 1904, (located in the Hoover Library) there is an article about a famous Sipiagin, Nikolai Martemyanovich (1785-1828), a Lieutenant General, who was highly decorated (including the Order of Saint George and diamond decorations of the Order of Saint Anne) and served in battles against Napoleon and against Turkey. Later he was appointed Military Governor of Tiflis (Tbilisi, Republic of Georgia) and was active in military events in the Caucasus.

Another distinguished member of the family was Dmitrii Sergeevich Sipiagin (1853-1902). In 1893 he was appointed governor of Moscow and served as a "gentleman in waiting" at the Royal Court, and then was Assistant Minister, under Czar Nikolas II. He was appointed to the ministry of Internal Affairs in 1894, and became head of the Ministry in 1899. He was assassinated by a member of the SR Party (Social Revolutionaries) in 1902.

Barbara's family, the Sipiagins, had a long history and existed in the XVI Century, at the time of Ivan-the-terrible. During that same century, the Sipiagin Crest was established.

Sipiagin Family Crest

SECTION THREE
My Wife Barbara's Family

Chapter 13: Barbara and the Cull Family

Barbara Jane (Cull) Jedenoff was born in Douglas, AZ on January 31, 1923. She had an older brother, John Porter Cull, Jr, born in 1920. Both of them were born in the family residence on 10th Street in Douglas, just ten blocks north of the border of Mexico and the town of Agua Prieta of Sonora, Mexico.

Barbara's father owned and operated a large cattle ranch about twenty miles northeast of Douglas. Although the ranch, the Bar M, contained an adequate ranch house, the family continued to live at their residence on 10th Street in Douglas. Barbara attended the Clawson Elementary School and began to display her talents and high intellect. She participated in many activities and was enrolled in a dancing school that taught her ballet and tap dancing. She participated in a number of recitals and programs at ages seven through ten.

Barbara was always a sweet and well-behaved child, and her father, who was fifty years older than her, often

Barbara at age nine

treated her as his pet. In his estimation she could do no wrong! This irked her brother who felt that he could never do anything right. Not surprising, some of this animosity continued into adult life.

Barbara entered Douglas High School in 1936, was a top student and was active in student affairs. At her graduation in 1939, she served as the class valedictorian. Her brother, John, also a good student, had graduated from Douglas High School a year earlier and then enrolled at Stanford. Their dad felt that Barbara should also attend Stanford where John could "keep an eye on her."

She entered Stanford in the fall of 1939, moving into Roble Hall, along with all the other frosh girls. In those days, it was mandatory for all frosh girls to reside their first year in Roble, while all freshmen boys were required to live in Encina Hall.

During the first year," Rushing" took place which gave all frosh students an opportunity to decide whether or not they wished to join a fraternity, sorority, or some other social residence for the balance of their stay at Stanford.

Barbara pledged Chi Omega Sorority and moved into that residence the following year as a sophomore. She was popular and had many dates. It was in that sophomore year that I, her future husband, was hired as a "hasher" (waiter) by her sorority while attending graduate school. For me, it was a case of "love at first sight" when I first saw her. She was not so sure! Thus I began a long and well planned conquest.

Barbara became active in her sorority and in her studies which were in the field of social studies, child psychology, and American history. She did well in these subjects but discovered that she had to work a lot harder than she did in high school. She served as a copy editor for the Stanford Daily newspaper and also for the annual publication, the year book, called "The Quad."

It may be of interest, that in those days, "Mexican food" was just becoming popular in the U.S. Barbara's mother was a very practical person and taught her daughter how to cook, sew, and tend to house-hold chores. Living so close to the Mexican border, Barbara became an expert in Mexican cuisine. Once her sorority sisters discovered her talent, they pleaded with her to prepare some Mexican food. After this first success, her cooking became so popular, that often her Mexican food was the "meal of the day." Given that many of her sorority sisters had been brought up differently (some had never been inside a kitchen), this gave Barbara an extra bit of respect and recognition from her sisters.

After long and steady persistence on my part, Barbara eventually became more interested and in early 1941, she accepted my fraternity pin; an indication of engagement. Later that year, on the evening of December 6, 1941, she accepted my proposal of marriage, little knowing that some fourteen hours later, Pearl Harbor would be bombed by the Japanese, thus precipitating World War II.

On February 27, 1943, we were married in the Stanford Chapel. Barbara selected her sorority roommate, Heddy Brockvogel as her maid of honor, and I selected my brother, Alexis, who was on active duty with the Marine Corps, to serve as best man.

Our wedding photo, February 27, 1943

After a short two-day honeymoon, Barbara went back to the Chi Omega house at Stanford to take her final exams, and I drove back to Pittsburg, CA to continue my work at the steel mill, pending receipt of orders to report for active duty with the Navy.

A month later I received these orders to report to the Naval Air Station at Quonset Point, Rhode Island for a concentrated indoctrination program. Barbara decided to go with me. Upon completion of my indoctrination I was assigned to report to a Navy office located at Douglas aircraft plant in El Segundo, California. After nine months I received orders to go overseas and Barbara returned to San Francisco to work for the Southern Pacific Railroad Company. She continued that work until I returned on December 30, 1945 after the war in the Pacific had come to an end.

I accepted employment with the steel mill in Pittsburg, CA. which was undergoing a huge modernization program at that time and was sent to other US Steel plants to learn how to operate the new equipment and Barbara accompanied me. From then on Barbara's life was pretty much integrated with mine. This involved moving to Provo UT, Gary IN, and Pittsburgh PA, and finally returning back to Orinda CA. Barbara was active raising our two children and supporting me in the busy social life associated with my being the head executive at each of the three steel plants, and with role as a corporate officer in the Pittsburgh headquarters of US Steel.

After I accepted the position of President of Kaiser Steel Company, we located in Orinda that was close to the Kaiser headquarters in Oakland and continued to live in that home for over forty years. During our married life we lived in twelve different homes, with none of those stays lasting over seven years, except for this last location.

Barbara passed away on May 11, 2018. We enjoyed over seventy-five years of a wonderful, happy marriage. During this time Barbara was most helpful to me. Her wise council and great sense of fairness were invaluable, and her loyal support was always an inspiration. She was truly my best friend.

Barbara's father, John Porter Cull, was a true Western pioneer. He was born in Cull Canyon (Hayward, CA), on March 26, 1873, the son of S. T. (Seaton Telford) and Minerva Cull who had eleven children, with John being number six. S.T. Cull was born in Kentucky and his roots trace back three generations to James Rubin Cull, who was born in England in 1735 and immigrated to the United States. In 1864, S.T. with three of his brothers, moved to California from Louisville, KY because they were sympathetic with the North during the Civil War.

John Porter Cull, 1930

John Cull's initial education was in a one-room schoolhouse which his father had built in the canyon after which he studied at a public school. After that he attended Lebanon College where he received business training. He was engaged in farming and cattle raising until 1897 when he decided to move to Wilcox, AZ which was then a major cattle raising area.He found employment in a general store where he learned the mercantile business and drove a team of horses to take supplies and the payroll to the local mines. After a few years, he moved to Bisbee and engaged in general merchandising in a partnership with a Mr. Anderson. He was successful in that enterprise but in January 1908 sold his interests and moved to Cortland, AZ where he bought property in the business district containing five store-rooms, and there he established a general mercantile store which he managed for many years. In1914, he bought a store in Douglas that he ran successfully until1920 when he decided to sell the business. In 1917, he bought a cattle ranch near Douglas, and three years later he purchased an adjacent and larger ranch which then provided him with his primary occupation.

One of John Cull's best friends, Fred Moore, was a rancher near Douglas, and encouraged him to get into the ranching business. Fred used to recall how John, to whom he jokingly referred to as a "tenderfoot," because of his late entry into the cattle business, taught him a trick or two about outdoor living. Once when they needed a fire to brand a calf and had no matches, John took out his six shooter and fired into some whittling and fanned the few sparks into a fire a trick he learned as a boy in Cull Canyon.

John Cull was one of the best-known citizens of Douglas. In 1919, he was elected to the lower house of the state Legislature and so satisfactory was his service in that body that two years later he was elected to the state Senate. He was again returned to the Senate during the difficult depression years of 1931 1932. In 1935, he was elected to the Board of Directors of the Bank of Douglas, a post which he held for two decades until his resignation two weeks before his death in 1955.

John Cull was truly an outstanding individual. He exhibited the traits that society emulates. He was dependable and honest to the core often referred to as "Honest John." He set a wonderful example for his children and fortunately they inherited and displayed those same traits. He never smoked and was a "teetotaler, never drinking alcohol except on the occasion of toasting an important agreement when he would drink a shot glass of beer. He believed that a man's word was his bond and many agreements were concluded by a handshake with an eye-to-eye exchange. Upon his death there were two significant declarations in his honor: one by the chairman of the Bank of Douglas; the other, a resolution in the 22nd legislature of the Senate of the state of Arizona. John Cull was the kind of pioneer that made our country great.

Chapter 14: Barbara's Mother and the Henningers

Georgina Henninger Cull, mother of Barbara and John, was born in San Diego, September 13, 1890. Her father, George William Henninger was born in Baden, Germany, in February 1850, and her mother, Wilhelmina (Minnie) Henninger Jahn was born in Nassau, Germany in March 1852. They immigrated to Hutchison, KS, where they lived until 1887. From there they moved their family to a fruit ranch in San Diego where Georgina was born. The family moved again to Bisbee, AZ in 1901, and lived there for the ensuing twenty years. George Henninger owned and operated a cigar factory and a hotel in Bisbee.

Brother George and sister Georgina

Georgina was their seventh female child. Her Dad was the third consecutive "George" in their family hierarchy, and the parents desperately wanted a son whom they could name George. After a string of seven daughters her father became frustrated and named his last one "Georgina." Lo and behold, his next child was a boy so they finally had a "George" after all. As an example of how methodical Germans are, four of their children were born on a September 13! Georgina, having moved to Bisbee when she was three, spent her youth in that city, attending public schools and working with her siblings in their dad's cigar factory. The Henninger clan was quite close knit and kept in close touch with each other over the years.

After Georgina married John Cull in 1919, the senior Henningers decided to move to Douglas, and settled about two blocks from the Cull residence. Georgina's mother passed away in 1928, and her dad developed ill health which put the burden of caregiving on his youngest daughter.

Georgina was very busy raising two children and caring for her ill father. She was an excellent mother and brought up her kids to be good students and to acquire the personal traits of loyalty, honesty, industry and respect. After her father passed away and her children went off to college, Georgina had time to develop some of her own talents. She was always interested in oil painting and was fortunate to be able to take lessons from a distinguished Western painter, Mrs. A. Y. (Effie) Smith. She was one of her most successful pupils and specialized in local desert scenery and flora. Having completed over forty oil paintings, she rewarded her family and relatives with these much-appreciated gifts.

Over the years Georgina Cull was active in local affairs, such as the YWCA, public school committees and community projects. In 1939 she became a charter member and ultimately president of a very interesting group called the "Cowbelles," which consisted of the wives of ranchers in the vicinity. Cattle folk love to visit and dance and swap old yarns, so while the purpose of the organization was purely social, to cement good will and friendship among wives and mothers of cattlemen in Cochise County, the members started immediately to make afghans and quilts for the Arizona children's home in Tucson. This they did while they visited and exchanged recipes, etc. After receiving some excellent publicity in the Arizona Cattle Growers weekly newsletter, requests came in from neighboring states to borrow the club's name and to establish similar clubs in their communities. Within a few years twenty-eight states established similar organizations a great idea which started in Douglas, Arizona.

Georgina Cull visiting the Canadian Rockies

Georgina Cull was a very generous person. After her husband died and she had more time, she engaged in her favorite activity traveling. She made many journeys, always inviting one of her sisters to go along as her guest. She continued her travels until she developed health problems.

Georgina Cull was a solid citizen, always supportive, and a very devoted mother. She died in Douglas, AZ in June of 1986 at the age of ninety-five. She was a very fine woman, and we are so grateful to her and for her legacy.

SECTION FOUR
Appendix

A: Vignettes of My Life

1: Crossing Siberia 1919

We made the long rail trip across Siberia to our destination of Vladivostok on the east coast, and we were quite comfortable in a private railroad car assigned to my dad. In Siberia, railroads provided the principal mode of travel since roads were very primitive and often not connecting. River traffic was also important where there were rivers.

Somewhere along our journey, Dad's private car was confiscated by our (White Army) forces because our troops needed more rolling stock to support their combat.

Sometime later, our train was stopped and taken over by the rebel Red forces, and still later the royalists White forces recaptured the train, only to lose it again several days down the road. Each time the rebels took over, all the passengers were searched and robbed. My mother prepared for this. My Brother Alex, about eight, and I about two at that time, each had a large teddy bear to travel with. Mom had cut open the teddy bears and hid jewelry, money and valuables inside them. The scheme worked well for a while until one Communist approached us and retorted, "How come your kids have two bears and my kid doesn't have any?" With that he grabbed one of the bears and went off with it. There went one half of mother's wealth!

2: Dad's Escape in Siberia 1919

While making our long trip across Siberia heading for Vladivostok, as mentioned, our train was captured several times by the rebels. On one occasion while White forces were trying to recapture the train, the engineer operating the locomotive was killed. A Bolshevik soldier, armed with a machine gun, went through the cars trying to find someone who could operate the locomotive. He came upon the four of us and questioned my dad. Papers he had indicated Dad's education as a mechanical engineer, specializing in railroads. The gunman knew that anyone getting that degree would have to know how to operate a locomotive. He ordered my dad, with the gun pointed at him, to advance to the locomotive to move the train. Dad got the locomotive morning and the train got underway, but he suspected that once we reached the next destination he would be shot. After a few miles the train proceeded over a bridge that crossed a deep gully. Dad was familiar with the location and halfway across the bridge he distracted the gunman, and at that point jumped out of the cab and into what he remembered to be a small stream. He did not realize that during this dry season, the stream was just a dry gully! He said he was so scared that he didn't even hurt himself when he landed.

Meanwhile the train rolled on for a while then finally came to a stop. Shortly thereafter

the White army came and recaptured the train. My mother, brother, and I were dispatched for shelter in a hut at the next village. Some four days later, my Dad found his way to the village and our family was reunited again.

3: Living in Harbin, 1921

With my dad in Harbin, 1921

I can remember at age three or four, walking with my Dad on the streets of Harbin. I remember lots of traffic mostly on foot. On the street corners there often were wooden huts one-person structures much like small outhouses. These provided some shelter in that harsh winter climate for soldiers who also served as policemen. I can remember one such soldier, harsh looking, dressed in a long khaki colored wool overcoat. He had his rifle with a bayonet mounted at his side. Many such soldiers expected an occasional tip to ensure that you would be safe.

Security in Harbin was always very unreliable. There was lots of graft, corruption, and a lack of any discipline. Gangs and individual bandits often prevailed. It paid to tip off the soldier-policeman.

I remember at one time seeing on the crowded streets a strange sight. There were pairs of people with faces covered with nose masks. They were carrying something prone, covered with a white sheet. I later learned that these men were carrying a dead body–someone who had just died from cholera. Harbin in 1920 22 had one of the most severe cholera epidemics on record and lost thousands of its population. Bodies were carried through the streets to a city dump where the corpses were burned. Cholera is highly infectious and our family was fortunate to have lived through the epidemic. Obviously, because of general security, the cholera epidemic, and the complete chaos in the region, I was on the streets very seldom only when necessity required. All in all these were not very pleasant memories, but then think of the worries and concerns my parents had about the safety of their two sons.

4: Almost in the Grasp

Nanna, my rescuer, in Harbin

While living in Harbin the Chinese-Eastern RR Company provided us with a nice large house that had a fenced-in backyard where I could play. One afternoon, while I was

playing, I looked up and saw a Chinese man scaling the fence. He was halfway over and called to me. I became very frightened, screamed, and ran full speed toward the back door. By that time the intruder was almost at my side.

Fortunately, our maid (Nanna) heard me, opened the door and grabbing my hand pulled me just out of the grasp of the intruder. She slammed the door shut and dropped the hinged security bar in place. It was customary at that time to equip all outside doors with such security bars for added protection.

To this day I can still visualize the intruder's hands as he was attempting to grab me. I would've provided him with a pretty decent ransom.

5: Santa Barbara, 1921

By early 1920, the revolution in Russia was widespread. The chief opposition and supporter of the royalists or White regime was Admiral Alexander Kulchak whose headquarters were in Siberia. In 1920 his protective guards, who were Czech soldiers, turned against him for they had been bought off by the Red regime, and they allowed Kulchak to be captured. He was promptly executed and his cache of some thirty to fifty million dollars in gold bullion, which were the funds being used to finance the resistance of the White army, was confiscated.

Being stationed in Harbin, Manchuria, my dad realized that the end of the White regime was close at hand. He considered emigrating to America, but since he knew very little about the U.S A. he decided that mother, with the two kids, should travel to to America to see what it was like. Consequently, mom along with Alexis and me, took the long journey to America. We first arrived in San Francisco, then took the train to Santa Barbara. An American friend, a Doctor Williams, whom mom and dad had met in Russia, invited us to visit him in Santa Barbara. We stayed in America for about 4 months. I was three or four when we were visiting in Santa Barbara, and there are a few things I can remember. My mother was fluent in speaking French and German.

One of the friends she made in California was a French lady about mom's age. They loved to converse in a language I could not understand. I used to hate it when the two women would get together because I was being neglected and left out of the conversation. I can remember several times when my Mom and I would be walking down the street in Santa Barbara, not a very big downtown in those days, and mom would realize I was pulling her over to one side, perhaps into a store. Then in a few minutes she would spot her French friend walking toward us. I spotted her first and tried to get mom out of the way before they actually saw each other. This happened several times – Mom would get a kick out of it, but to me it was a calamity for I never liked that French lady.

I remember many happy days spent on the beach at Santa Barbara: I loved to play in the sand and wade out in the water. Mom always dressed me in sailor suits, and we have lots of pictures of me dressed that way. I was a towhead and always had a smile, except when mom's French lady friend would show up that is!

One of my fond memories is how I learned to read in English. I loved the funny papers, and I looked forward to Sundays when the full section of funnies appeared. I think one of my very first words in English was "funny papers."

On the beach in Santa Barbara

Interestingly enough, shortly after we left Santa Barbara to return to China, Santa

Barbara experienced the very devastating earthquake of 1921, and much of the city was destroyed. We were fortunate to have left for China by then.

6: Retro 1930 High Tech

After all four of us had moved permanently to America, my parents separated and Alexis lived with my Dad in a small apartment in Seattle Washington while I lived with my Mom in another apartment not far away, but I would spend time with each of my parents.

One day Dad told me to expect a surprise that evening. Alexis and I waited patiently until Dad came home from work. He arrived – and his surprise was a gadget called a "crystal set," which was the forerunner of the radio. It was a strange looking unit consisting of a silver sparkling rock which was the crystal and a small needle that was mounted with a flexible wire connector to a little box attached to which was an ear phone that you placed on one ear while you moved the needle around on the crystal until you got a sound. You adjusted the needle to get the clearest sound possible so you could pick up a broadcast from one of several radio stations.

That night there was a world championship boxing match, and it was exciting to hear it being broadcast through the air without wires or anything! We took turns listening to the broadcast. What a marvelous development we thought. Imagine that sound being transmitted through "thin air," and we could hear someone talking from miles away! "What will they think of next?" we thought. (And here I am, writing all this on my iPhone!)

7: My First Visit to Stanford

June 1940, with my happy mother

One Sunday in 1934, while I was still attending Polytechnic High School in San Francisco, my mother and stepdad decided to take a sightseeing drive to the Stanford University campus which they had never visited before. I came along for the ride and instantly fell in love with the campus. I said to my mother, "Wow, would I love to be able to attend a school like this!" My always-positive mother looked me in the eye and said, "Son, someday you will attend Stanford." I was accustomed to my mother's optimism but this statement just threw me. Knowing how poor we were and how we struggled for a living, this statement was just too much. I flared up and in an angry mood criticized her for building false hopes by asserting such an incredible prediction. In fact I was so upset that I didn't speak to her for several days.

Lo and behold, in June 1940, my parents attended and witnessed my graduation ceremony at Stanford!

8: An Incident at the Bald Eagle Mines

During the summer of 1936, I was able to get employment as a "mucker" at the Bald Eagle Mines, thanks to the Stanford Alumni Association.

Paul Durckel on the right

The mining camp where we lived was located in a canyon, and the one road that entered the canyon was the only flat space available. Since my friend Paul Durckel and I wanted to play football, we used to practice on this one flat road. We would kick a football and pass to each other and try to get in the best shape possible.

The only real problem we had at the camp was that the food quality was marginal at best. For a couple of growing kids we just didn't get enough decent stuff to eat and since we paid a dollar and a half out of the four dollars we earned, which is a pretty high percentage, we felt gypped. One evening Paul and I felt particularly hungry so we decided to raid the kitchen to get something to eat. While we were in the kitchen, the chef, a questionable character at best, discovered our presence and confronted us. He picked up a meat cleaver and charged after us. Because of my size, I figured my best defense was to use my legs and to get the hell out of there. Paul, being a lineman and a pretty good-sized guy decided to hold his ground and as the chef came after him with the cleaver Paul smacked him and beat him up pretty well. All this commotion brought others to the scene.

The next day the mine superintendent held a hearing, and we were sure we were going to lose our jobs. We told the superintendent why this occurred, and a number of the miners came to our rescue and confirmed that the food was indeed terrible. Fortunately for us, the mine superintendent acknowledged the problem, fired the cook, and assured us that we would have better meals. Shortly thereafter, we got a new cook who provided us with much better food, so instead of our being fired, our act of defiance was applauded by the miners who also became beneficiaries of the improved meals.

9: House Manager at the Fraternity

As at most fraternities the Phi Kappa Psi fraternity was managed by a house manager, who is elected by the members. I was elected house manager in my junior year and served two continuous one-year terms. When I took over, the fraternity was in debt and the finances were not in very good shape. I was determined to get ourselves out of debt and to operate on a break-even basis. The paid staff reporting to the manager was a cook and his wife, and a houseboy who cleaned the rooms, made up the beds, and performed general handiwork. All three employees had rooms in the house. My first task was to establish budgets and to ensure that the income from the members matched the expenses for running the house. Several of the members were delinquent in their payments because they would spend the money they received from home on other items before they paid the rent. On a case-by-case basis we resolved the delinquency and set up a schedule whereby the member would pay his rent immediately as he received his check from home.

This took some close surveillance, but gradually the process began to work. At the same time I had to take a close look at our expenses and to reduce them wherever possible. Heating expenses were high so I initiated a campaign to use our heat more efficiently and set the thermostat to a lower temperature.

Chris making beds on the Phi Kappa Psi sleeping porch

Most fraternities had guest nights when they could bring girlfriends and their buddies to dinner. One guest night I came down to the dinner table with just a T-shirt on, but all the members and their guests had their scarves and overcoats on and sat there shivering to dramatically indicate to me that it was cold, and I had gone too far. After that we did raise the thermostat a bit!

Another big expense item was for food, especially for desserts. One cheap dessert that we relied on quite heavily was Jell-O. Again, on one occasion of protest, all the brothers broke into a boisterous rendition of the Jell-O commercial. But after taking these drastic steps we did manage to break even and at the end of the first year we were out of debt. The brothers appreciated this but never stopped needling me for my draconian efforts to save money.

Our houseboy, Chris Madarang, a tiny Filipino weighing about 100 pounds was a real fixture in the house. The brothers loved to tease him. One of our brothers, Tiff Denton, was the son of the world's billiards champion. When Tiff joined the fraternity, his dad donated a beautiful pool and billiard table to the house which created a very popular activity for the brothers. In his spare time, which was substantial, Chris learned how to play billiards and became very proficient. He delighted challenging the brothers and would spot them a big head start, but he was always the winner. This was one way he had to get even with the teasing he was receiving and to pick up some extra change.

When World War II started, Chris got a job at the Mare Island Naval shipyard, and it is rumored that because of his small size, he was able to get inside the torpedo tubes used on submarines to polish up the internal surfaces.

10: How I Met Barbara, 1940

Barbara at the Chi Omega sorority

When I entered graduate school, I no longer had the benefit of a generous scholarship nor the financial benefits of being house manager which I had enjoyed in my latter undergrad days. I had to find a "hashing job" (waiter) to provide for my meals. The most desirable jobs were in the girls sorority houses. When I was house manager at the Phi Psi house, I belonged to a university commissary that purchased food for all of the Stanford eating clubs and units. Through this association I became friends with Lizzie, the housemother of the Chi Omega sorority. I approached her and asked if I could get a hashing job at her sorority. She told me that that decision had to be made by the girls themselves, but she would be pleased to put in a good word for me with the president of the sorority, Elaine Stone. I phoned Elaine and took her out for a date. I asked her for the job and my request was granted.

As hashers our task was to set up the tables, serve the meals (lunch and dinner), clean up the dining room, and wash the dishes, with partial help from an old dishwasher.

The Chi Omegas had wonderful cooks – a nice black couple named Aaron and

Virginia, and they made the greatest corn or "co'n" bread. Everything went well that first fall quarter of 1940, but then the girls started to complain about putting on too much weight. Their solution was to cut back on the lunches and serve only salads. This was great for the girls, but for us growing young men we needed something more substantial. We almost went on strike, but knowing we could not win, we just adjusted and griped among ourselves.

In those days at Stanford, all incoming frosh lived in university dormitories: the boys in Encina Hall and the girls in Roble Hall. Toward the end of the first year, the fraternities and sororities had "rushing" which was a process of inviting frosh to their respective clubs and ultimately inviting those whom they wanted to join their respective fraternities or Sororities. Those who were invited and who accepted were called pledges.

The new pledges moved into their respective units the following year as sophomores. In the fall of 1940, I started hashing at the Chi Omega Sorority House. Of course we had more than just a casual interest in the girls who we served, especially those young, innocent, sweet sophomore pledges.

At one dinner while serving, I spotted a cute young sophomore who really appealed to me right at first sight. I was waiting for an opportune moment and finally, while serving tea, I looked at her and inquired, "Sugar?" She was a bit startled, then I offered her some sugar but she knew full well what I was implying. That was my first introduction to Barbara and look what that little incident has led us to!

Sometime in the fall of 1940, I finally got around to asking Barbara for a date. The big events in those days were "hotel dancing" to the Big Bands in San Francisco. Barbara and I double dated with my good friend, Eddie DeMoss, and his date. He drove and Barbara and I were in the backseat. We had a great time and really enjoyed the music and each other. On the way home I fell asleep, and while this should have been fair warning to Barbara about my future behavior, fortunately she didn't let that interrupt our relationship.

11: "Our" Professor, 1910 and 1940

One of my favorite professors at Stanford was Stephan Timoshenko who taught the basic engineering course called "Strength of Materials." He was a very famous engineer with many international honors for his technical contributions. It was quite a coincidence that Prof. Timoshenko earned the rank of full professor at the Kiev Polytechnic Institute, and in 1907 was my Dad's professor in engineering when Dad was a student in Russia. After leaving Russia for America in 1923, Timoshenko worked in engineering and research for Westinghouse Electric Company, but after several years he decided that he preferred teaching and in 1927 was appointed professor of engineering at the University of Michigan where he wrote the "bible" on the subject of strength of materials. In 1936 he was recruited by Stanford and joined the engineering faculty.

As an undergrad I took several courses from "Timi," as he was called, and greatly

Monument honoring Prof. Stephan Timoshenko: at Kiev Polytechnic Institute

appreciated his intellect and teaching ability. When I was in graduate school, I had difficulty meeting my financial obligations and needed part time work.

It so happened that in 1940, Timoshenko decided to revise and update his textbook, and he needed someone to edit the printed draft of his book. I was hired to do this and had the opportunity of meeting with Timi quite often always a rewarding experience. He became aware of the fact that he was teacher to both father and son. When the first edition of his new book was published, he wrote in my copy, "To my two pupils, Alexander N Jedenoff, 1907, and George A Jedenoff, 1940 – 25th of September 1940, S. Timoshenko."

Prof. Timoshenko was honored by many groups and professional associations because of his international stature. In his honor, Kiev Polytechnic Institute erected a fifteen-foot statue of him on the campus grounds. In 2004, I visited Kiev (now in Ukraine) and had the opportunity to visit the college and was able to have a picture taken next to Timi's statue.

12: No Bull, 1945

Guamanian farmer's most valued possession

While stationed on Guam I was assigned a Jeep because I was head of my unit. It was a typical stripped-down wartime Jeep, manual shift and all-wheel drive, but with no other features, not even a windshield wiper which made it interesting driving on a rainy day over un-paved dirt roads. But at least I had wheels for my professional and personal needs. One Sunday, I invited my Graduate School of Business classmate, George Parker, who was a Marine officer stationed on the other side of the island, to go exploring with me and to visit some of the native villages.

On the way back to our base we spotted a dirt road that ran across a cultivated field. It had rained recently but since my Jeep had all-wheel drive I was not concerned about crossing the field. About halfway through, the road became quite soft and muddy, but no worry—four-wheel drive. But alas, the Jeep got mired in the mud! The more I tried to maneuver out, the deeper we went. After a while we became concerned for it was getting late and there were still a lot of Japanese soldiers loose on the island.

Suddenly, we noticed some movement at the far end of the cultivated field, undoubtedly alerted by the noise we were making. Were these friends or foes? George and I drew our revolvers and were ready to at least put up a fight, but in a few seconds we realized that we had spotted a native farmer, accompanied by his huge caribou or water buffalo. He waved in a friendly fashion, and we directed him to advance. He quickly sized up the mess we were in and offered to help us out. We were obviously happy to get help. The farmer directed his caribou to get behind the Jeep and with a powerful push by this huge animal the Jeep just shot out of the hole it was in. We were so grateful to the farmer and his valuable helper, and that's no bull.

13: Our Trip to Mexico, 1946

Our reliable (?) Wartime Ford

I was still in the Naval reserve having come back home on December 30, 1945, and waiting to be released from the Navy. But first I had to use up about six weeks of cumulative leave. Barbara and I decided to visit Mexico which at that time was very anxious to encourage its tourism business. We took our Ford clunker which was about a 1937 vintage and decided to take the new Trans-American Highway which ran from Laredo, Texas through Monterey into Mexico City and beyond. I was still technically in uniform. We drove to Douglas, AZ to visit the senior Culls, and then on to Laredo, TX. Our car was still equipped with recap tires since new tires were not yet available to the general public. We were assured by the Mexican Tourist Bureau that we would have tires available, new or retread, if we needed them. From Laredo we drove south into Mexico.

We had reservations in Monterey at a Hotel Favorita, wherever that was. We looked frantically for the hotel once we got to Monterey. On the street I spotted a well-dressed Mexican gentleman who appeared to know a few words of English. I asked him if he knew where Hotel Favorita was. "Si", he said, but he could not direct me with his limited English, so he said he would go with us and show us the way. As we drove along, at each intersection he would say "Alto, Stop" then we would proceed. The wild drivers in Mexico made him nervous. Finally we found the Favorita, and I thanked him and wanted to tip him for his trouble, but he refused any money and just smiled and walked away.

The Favorita was an old but quite nice hotel, and our room was on the second floor overlooking the main street. All was well until we discovered that that evening was a holiday and the whole town would be celebrating. We were almost certain that the entire populace had gathered out in front of our hotel loud music and singing all night long. We had driven all day and were really tired, but as tired as we were, we were still kept awake all night. Since then we've enjoyed a lot of laughs whenever "Hotel Favorita" is mentioned.

14: Visiting Grandma, 1960

About 1958, my mother and my step-dad, Georgi Ivanovich, moved back from San Carlos to San Francisco into the Sunset District, a misnomer because of the summer fog, they never saw the sun. Our son Nick was about five. Mom invited us to dinner, and she treated us with a Russian dish called "pelimeni." Nick asked what we were eating and when we said "pelimeni " he thought that was hysterical for it was such a musical sounding word to him. He burst out in a joyous laughter and started running all over the house, shouting "pelimeni, pelimeni, pelimeni!" He loved the name more than he liked the taste of the product. We have laughed over that incident many times.

Along the beach in Santa Barbara, 1958, Nick age 5, Nina age 2

15: Who's to Blame? 1959

At US Steel, one of the perks afforded to plant managers and other executives was the periodic visit for a complete physical checkup at one of several clinics. In about 1959, I selected Samsun Clinic in Santa Barbara for this four-day procedure. Barbara and I and our two young children were put up in one of the finer hotels. Dining in an elegant restaurant with two young children is always a challenge. Nick, in particular, was very active and we lectured to him about behaving properly.

At dinner one evening, everything was going quite smoothly when suddenly one of the waiters tripped and accidentally dropped his whole loaded tray. The crashing dishes made a giant disturbing roar.

At that point Nick jumped out of his chair and screamed at the top of his voice, "I didn't do it!" This amused all of the diners and eased an awkward situation.

16: A Mormon Christening, 1962

It was the summer of 1962, and our Geneva steel plant was experiencing a serious labor strike that was getting violent. Automobile tires were being slashed and there were other incidents of violence. For their safety, we sent Mom and our two children back to California to visit our parents. As the General Superintendent of the plant, my involvement was 24/7 alertness and the pressure was pretty great. One Saturday, my friend who was the public relations director in Salt Lake City, Art McQuiddy, called me and suggested that I get away from the stress for a short while and suggested that I come into Salt Lake City to have dinner with him and his assistant, Dave Bigler. Dave had membership in the newly redecorated Fort Douglas Country Club and invited Art and me to be his guest for dinner and relaxation.

After a few drinks and a lovely dinner we decided to walk around the club to see the new additions which included a brand-new swimming pool. It was a very warm evening and we were strolling around the grounds at about ten. Dave made a comment about it being hot and that he had on this cool seersucker suit, and he made the unfortunate mistake of saying that it was washable. The power of suggestion took over as Dave was standing near the edge of the pool glancing at the water. Suddenly, he received a gentle shove from one of us and he was in the water, clothes and all. None of us were feeling any regret, but at that moment Dave laughed and exclaimed, "Man, it's really nice and cool in here." In an instant, Art and I stripped down to our underwear and decided to join Dave in the pool. Art climbed up on the high diving board and he was quite a sight, for all he had on was a pair of very baggy boxer shorts, and as he dove into the water he looked like a sailboat under a full spinnaker! After we had hit the water, Dave, who was brought up as a Mormon, raised his right hand and proclaimed us as being christened into the Mormon faith. So Dave got back at us in this indirect manner. Incidentally, David Bigler was the great grandson of the first governor of the state of California. In fact the giant lake adjacent to the state of Nevada was originally named Lake Bigler, but later, the name was changed to Lake Tahoe. Several days after this incident, Dave received a letter from the Manager of the Fort Douglas Country Club telling him that he was not welcome to bring such boisterous guests to the club ever again.

17: And for Dessert? 1963

Utah is a beautiful state, and when we resided there we often visited some of its many scenic places. One summer day we were traveling through Saint George in southern Utah at about lunchtime. We spotted what seemed to be an appropriate restaurant and ordered our lunch. The waitress asked us what we wanted for dessert. Nina spotted some freshly baked pies and pointed to one and said, "I'll have a piece of that glueberry pie". We all burst out in laughter, at Nina's expense. She was very embarrassed, but guess what? She was right. It was a terrible piece of pie and probably resembled a pie made with glue, rather than with blueberries

18: A Guardian Angel, 1964

The city of Provo, Utah is situated in a level valley and spreads up against the Wasatch Mountain Range which has many interesting and beautiful canyons. Some of these canyons are quite rustic and still very primitive with access only via an unpaved dirt road. Often on Sundays, after attending church service, we would drive into one of these canyons to enjoy a picnic lunch and the solitude and beauty of the canyon. Within thirty or forty minutes from our house we could find ourselves in total wilderness.

One beautiful spring day we decided to enter one of the smaller canyons that we had not visited before. The only road into the canyon started out as a unpaved gravel road that gradually became less maintained and more primitive. At one point we had to ford a shallow but rocky creek. While crossing the stream we apparently struck a sharp rock that pierced the oil pan of the engine on our car. After driving a short distance the emergency light went on to warn us that we were not getting proper lubrication. I looked under the car and sure enough, oil had escaped through a hole in the punctured oil pan. I was sure that the engine would burn up before we got very far, and since this was the age before mobile cell phones we were at a loss as to what to do next. It was really too far to hike out but that looked like the only solution to this unfortunate situation. Before long it would get dark and the ambient temperature would get cold, and undoubtedly there were still some wild animals that lived in the canyon.

Nonetheless since the children were about six to eight years of age, we decided that they and Barbara would stay in the car, and I would hike out as fast as I was able.

Just about that time, low and behold and almost out of the blue a Jeep appeared. It seems that there was an organization of people who spent their Sundays patrolling the canyons in order to spot anyone who might be in trouble—a group of true "guardian angels." The driver of the Jeep said that he had spotted me and figured that I was in trouble. He inspected the damaged tank and noticed that I was wearing a leather belt. He cut a piece out of the belt, took a nail from his car and repaired the leak by plugging up the hole with the nail and leather patch. He carried spare cans of oil and used one of them for the crankcase. "There," he said, "there is enough oil in your crankcase to get you to a service station."

After thanking him profusely I tried to pay him, but he would not take any money. He said he was a good Mormon but instead of going to church on Sundays he would express his devotion by trying to help people who might be in trouble. Every weekend he and his group would patrol the various canyons of the Wasatch Range in order to spot people who might be having difficulties. What a wonderful way to demonstrate one's faith and religion!

19: A Lesson on the Ski Slopes, 1980

With Junior Bounous at Snowbird

One beautiful sunny day, my good friend Junior Bounous and I were skiing at Snowbird on a neatly groomed slope. We stopped midway on the run, and Junior said to me "Come on, George, follow me." Junior headed for an area that was not groomed and was just horrible crud. "What are we doing, Junior? This is terrible, I can't ski it," I exclaimed.

"Sure you can, George, I will show you how," he replied. After a few difficult attempts, I finally got the hang of it and was able to ski even under these lousy conditions. Junior laughed and said, "Great, George! You know every day is not going to be a beautiful sunny day like this nor is the run going to be nicely groomed like it is today. So what are you going to do? Go sit in the lodge, mope around and complain about the poor ski conditions, or be a real skier who can have fun regardless of the situation?"

This was a valuable lesson in attitudes and it is applicable to life itself. A lesson that I have never forgotten.

20: A Hand Simile

In our effort to obtain greater employee participation and more effective teamwork I found it most important that we all understood what our mission was.

Although a great oversimplification I used the hand to illustrate what we were trying to accomplish. Basically everyone in our plant had the same tasks to perform, whether it was a crew member or the General Superintendent of the plant. In order to make it easier to grasp and to remember, I used the hand as a symbol. A hand contains five fingers which can work independently of each other but when coordinated properly

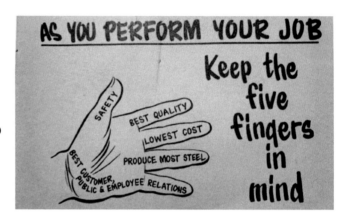

they make the strongest hand possible. Our occupational duties fall into five categories, each represented by a separate finger. These are: safety, quality, costs, productivity, and relationships.

Consequently our mission is to properly coordinate these functions so that we can:

> "safely, with the best quality, at the lowest cost, produce the most units, with the best customer, public, employee, an environmental relations."

Just like the fingers of the hand that move independently of each other, they must be properly balanced to obtain the strongest grip possible. Likewise, in performing our duties the five management functions must be properly balanced. Over stressing any one of the functions may result in weakening of other functions. For instance, high productivity cannot be emphasized over quality and safety, and so forth…

It was our objective to make all of our employees cognizant of these factors and to realize that in the performance of their jobs a proper balance of all five fingers must be attained. After having discussions of these factors with all employees, a card similar to the one illustrated was issued to each member of our team. Since everyone is constantly aware of his hands, this simile served as a constant reminder of the total responsibility that each of us has.

This better understanding of our mission was helpful in obtaining improved performance of our plant.

B: Testimonials

DESERET
NEWS

6-14-67

Thanks, Mr. Jedenoff

When George A. Jedenoff, general superintendent of U.S. Steel's Geneva Works, moves to Gary, Ind., to become general manager of the plant there, Utah County will lose one of its most outstanding boosters.

Among his accomplishments have been successful work not only in his own company, which has seen a notable rise in production and stability, but also in education, industrial development, the United Fund, his own church, the Provo Chamber of Commerce, the Utah Manufacturers Assn., and the Boy Scouts — to list but a few of his associations.

For his many services, Brigham Young University last year honored him with the Jesse Knight Citizenship Award.

That Mr. Jedenoff has been promoted to the U.S. Steel plant at Gary — more than four times the size of the Geneva Works — is an indication of his ability and achievements. Gary's gain will be Utah County's loss.

We express appreciation to Mr. Jedenoff for his industry and imagination in helping to build Utah, particularly Utah County, and wish him and his family success in their move.

KSL EDITORIAL

(157-'66)

GENEVA   AIRED: Week of November 14, 1966

Problems can be stumbling blocks or stepping stones, depending on the kind
of man who faces them. And, of course, the difference is the difference
between failure and success.

The Geneva Works of U. S. Steel has faced some imposing problems. Located
in the Great Basin, it has lacked big local markets. The great bulk of its
production must be shipped elsewhere, mostly to the West Coast, and rail
freight rates are so high it is cheaper to ship from the East Coast to
California than from Utah to California. Increasing competition from fully
integrated steel plants on the coast, to say nothing of Japan, has put the
Utah plant under tremendous pressure.

Some men or companies might crumble under such pressure. But George Jedenoff, Geneva's general superintendent, and his staff are not such men. They
saw their problems as a challenge to grow. Last year, Geneva's 6,000 workers
joined with Mr. Jedenoff in the "Errors Zero" program. They pledged to overcome Geneva's natural obstacles by superior production, eliminating the mistakes and indifference that add so much to a company's costs.

At the same time, the company, together with Utah officials, kept hammering
away for lower freight rates -- and finally won.

This week came the payoff. Mr. Jedenoff announced a multi-million-dollar
expansion program that will add 500 jobs to the area's payroll.

The program should substantially improve Geneva's competitive position, as
well as stimulate the Utah economy.

Overcoming problems builds men and companies and nations.

KSL salutes Geneva Steel for using its problems as stepping stones.

KSL RADIO AND KSL TELEVI
BROADCAST H(
SALT LAKE CITY, UTAH

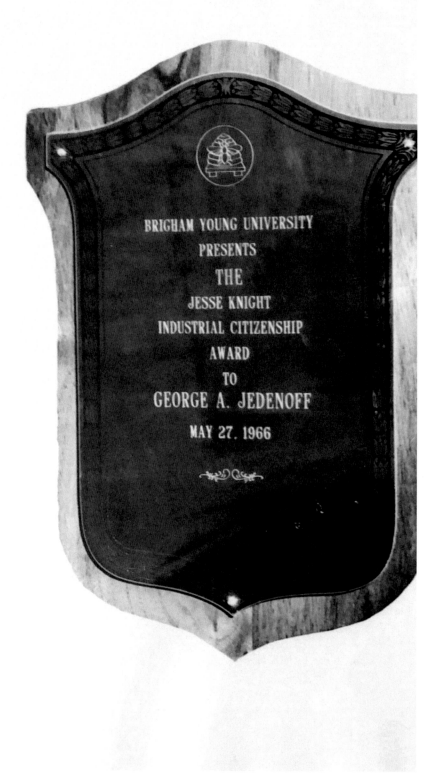

Awards—BYU Jesse Knight Industrial Citizenship Award. May 27, 1966

The Daily Herald

**Dedicated to the Progress And
Growth of Central Utah**

WEDNESDAY, JUNE 14, 1967

Jedenoff's Imprint on Valley

Central Utahns will say goodbye to George A. Jedenoff with mixed emotions.

Congratulations are due him on his new appointment as general superintendent of the Gary Work of U.S. Steel. But it'll be hard for the people to be genuinely enthusiastic about a promotion that will take him away from Utah Valley where he has done such a monumental job as general superintendent of the Geneva Works.

Mr. Jedenoff, who came here after tenure as general superintendent of the corporation's Pittsburg Works in California, was for Geneva and Utah Valley all the way.

He sensed what others had known—that our Utah Valley steel mill was in jeopardy due to growing competitive challenges from foreign and domestic producers.

More important, he undertook with great vigor and courage, to do something about the problem.

With the help of able assistants in the steel industry, the cooperation of the Geneva employees, and the backing of the community and state, he spearheaded a crusade for efficiency and economy of operations, increased customer service, improved freight rates, and more aggressive sales program that has kept Geneva competitive as a producer.

A great booster for Utah Valley, Mr. Jedenoff has projected himself into community life. Among other things he was instrumental in establishment of the Utah Valley Industrial Development Association which is working for new payrolls and industrial growth.

His positive attitude, farsightedness, and "can-do" spirit regardless of the dimensions of the task, have helped to keep both Geneva and the valley moving.

When he leaves Geneva July 1 to manage U.S. Steel's largest mill at Gary, Mr. Jedenoff will leave a large pair of shoes to fill. Utah Valley will miss him. But in a geared-up steel operation and his many civic contributions he has given us something tangible and valuable to remember him by.

SALT LAKE TRIBUNE
Salt Lake City, Utah
June 16, 1967

Utah Loses Good Man in George Jedenoff

While George A. Jedenoff of Utah's Geneva Steel Works must be congratulated on his promotion to head U.S. Steel's largest mill at Gary, Indiana, The Tribune cannot but express regret at Utah's loss of a man whose dynamic leadership and good citizenship had come to be greatly admired in the few years he has been with us.

George Jedenoff came to Utah in 1960 as general superintendent of the Geneva Works. Since then he has served a dual role of helping to pull the Geneva operation up, in effect, by its bootstraps, to a better competitive position in West Coast markets, while he at the same time assumed a variety of positions of civic leadership in Provo, Utah County, and the state.

Mr. Jedenoff's campaign of Errors Zero, which enlisted the support of Geneva's 5,000 employes in superior individual and team performance, helped to compensate for Geneva's handicap in serving major West Coast markets at distances up to 900 miles from the mill. These efforts in turn had won from U.S. Steel important new investment for modernization and new facilities at Geneva.

Mr. Jedenoff has been promoted to be general superintendent of one of the largest and most diversified steelmaking plants — four times the size of Geneva — and we wish him well in his new assignment.

Meanwhile Utah awaits the arrival of Raymond W. Sundquist, now general superintendent of U.S. Steel's plant at Braddock, Pennsylvania, as Mr. Jedenoff's successor—confident that he will ably fill a rather large pair of shoes in both industry management and civic service.

WASHINGTON SUMMARY

United States Steel

PUBLIC RELATIONS: MIDDLE ATLANTIC DISTRICT • 1625 K STREET, N.W., WASHINGTON, D. C. 20006 / (202) 783-2000

Friday, September 18, 1970

ON THE INSIDE

CEDAR BAYOU, ROWLESBURG FUNDS APPROVED BY CONFEREES

ooooo

NON-RETURNABLE BEVERAGE CONTAINERS UNDER HOUSE EYE

ooooo

TRADE BILL REACHES SENATE IN LEGISLATIVE MANEUVER

JEDENOFF OF USS AT CAPITOL HILL "ZERO DEFECTS" MEET
\- - - - -
SEES ENCOURAGING RESULTS FROM USS PLANT EFFORTS
RELATES GENEVA WORKS "ERRORS ZERO" STORY
\- - - - - - - - - -

Several newly launched employee motivation efforts at U. S. Steel plants around the nation are beginning to show encouraging result and the approach is likely to spread within the corporation, industry and government leaders were told at a meeting here yesterday. The assessment came from George A. Jedenof general manager - heavy products operations, who was among participants at a day-long Capitol Hill conference on "Zero Defects" programs, sponsored by Rep. Charles S. Gubser (R., Calif.), a member of the House Armed Services Committee.

Jedenoff was general superintendent at Geneva Works in 1966, when the Utah plant launched its widely recognized "Errors Zero" program, a locally oriented derivative of the "Zero Defects" concept. He told the conference how Geneva's continued survival had been severely threatened by the growing invasion of foreign steel imports which hit West Coast markets during the 1960's. The response at the plant, he related, was to begin the highly localized motivational effort aimed at sharpening the mill's competitive muscle. This led ultimately to the beginning of "Errors Zero" at a mass meeting in 1966, attended by more than 8,500 customers, community and government leaders, plant employees and members of their families. He said the result at Geneva thus far has been the conver sion of a "complacent, labor-troubled mill into a model of competitive accomplishment" -- a plant that has continued to survive.

Jedenoff emphasized that the basis of the Geneva Works experience had been the belief that "well informed, dedicated employees -- operating as a team -- are the key to a successful, profitable operation." The "Errors Zero" approach was merely an organized means of sharing the plant's competitive responsibility through a "one team" philosophy in an effort that was "positive, objective, motivational, aggressive and, above all, local." Then, as competitive developments confronted other U. S. Steel plants throughou the country, Jedenoff stated that an attempt has been made to apply many of these principles elsewhere -- at such works as Gary, Texas, Christy Park, Joliet, Waukegan, Fairfield, Homestead, Clairton and Johnstown. He indicated that early results from the other mills had been encouraging. "Each effort reflects the leadership of the individua plant superintendent," he said. "As each superintendent begins to realize he can attair more profitable operation through the 'one team' effort, we are confident we will see a progressively greater use of the sound principles which underly the approach."

- 386 -

OVER

Says Programs Require Localization, Shared Responsibility

Jedenoff went on to say such motivational activities cannot be launched by pressing a set of buttons or pulling levers from on high. The key to all the U. S. Steel efforts has been that they are localized and geared to local competitive circumstances. Focus of the message at all the plants, he stated, "is on competition and the need for all employees to share the responsibility, of the plant and the overall company, to achieve an upward and improving rate of profitability in the face of the toughest competitive challenges in U. S. Steel's history. In line with this comes the realization that competition has to do with people and not machines, technology or systems."

"The aim is to debunk the thinking that a man who works in a steel mill isn't important; and instead create a plant-wide awareness that everyone who fills a necessary job, competing for customers at the best possible margin of profit, is vital to the total operation. It follows that, if the position is necessary, the man who fills it is far too important to simply punch a time clock and go through the motions. In fact, he is important enough to carry a full share of the duty to compete profitably for the growth and betterment of his plant and community."

Sees Management Leadership as Critical Element

Jedenoff went on to point out that management must recognize that results from such an approach may require considerable time and direction; that the local management must provide "solid leadership" in gaining the commitment of all employees to the "single team" philosophy. "As well, it falls to the management leader to be a communicator, maintaining a steady flow of information to the plant people and community -- factual reports on competitive gains and losses and objective interpretations of the economic stakes involved. It also imposes on the manager the discipline of listening, in order to generate and benefit from participation by all members of the plant team."

Remarks Praised by Pentagon, NASA Officials

The description by the U. S. Steel aide drew support from additional participants at the meeting, including Vice Admiral Eli T. Reich, Deputy Assistant Secretary of Defense for Material, and Phillip Bolger, director of NASA's motivational approaches surrounding the manned flight program. Reich said he agreed on the need for localizing all such motivational programs. He said he was flatly opposed to any approach wherein the Federal government, specifically the Defense Department, would establish some sort of "rigid superstructure" to tell industry how it spurs its people to better workmanship and greater competitive efforts. Bolger said his programs with NASA had attempted to make the same sort of approach outlined by Jedenoff. "If I wanted a good description of what we've been trying to do in the manned flight program it would be the one outlined by the gentleman from U. S. Steel -- almost word-for-word," he stated. (T. R. FERRALL)

CEDAR BAYOU, ROWLESBURG FUNDS APPROVED BY HOUSE-SENATE CONFEREES. House and Senate Public Works conferees yesterday approved a $60,000 appropriation for planning on the Cedar Bayou project in Texas, and $1.5 million in land acquisition funds for the Rowlesburg Dam project in West Virginia. The appropriations, involving projects closely linked to U. S. Steel plants, came as part of a $5.2 billion public works appropriation bill to fund Federal projects during the current fiscal year.

Cedar Bayou, an incomplete 100-foot wide adjunct of the Houston Ship Channel, would provide a needed waterway line for barge-shipped steel slabs out of U. S. Steel's Texas Works near Houston. The dredging of Cedar Bayou, a long-dormant program on the drawing boards since 1931, has been urged by Earl W. Mallick, U. S. Steel's vice-president South, in testimony earlier this year. It also had the backing of Texas government and business leaders. Funds for the planning stage approval contemplate dredging to the originally planned 10-foot channel depth.

KSL 5

GEORGE JEDENOFF   AIRED: June 28, 1967

Some people find that obstacles are stumbling blocks. Others use them as stepping stones. George Jedenoff is one of the latter.

When George came to Utah seven years ago, Geneva Steel Company was in trouble. Cut off from natural markets by distance and high freight rates, it faced tough competition from new integrated steel mills on the West Coast and in Japan. Moreover, it had been plagued by labor problems, including that most insidious problem, the slowdown.

Such problems could have killed Geneva and left Central Utah without one of its greatest economic assets. But George Jedenoff turned the problems into stepping stones. He faced the competition with aggressive modernization and expansion programs. He launched a man-to-man program of winning over the workers, culminating in the Errors Zero program in which Geneva's 5,000 worker have joined in an intensive drive for superior performance.

This is the kind of leadership that has brought Mr. Jedenoff an important appointment as General Superintendent of one of the country's largest and most diversified steel plants.....The U.S. Steel plant at Gary, Indiana. But it is not this achievement alone that has prompted his many friends to honor him at a testimonial dinner Thursday night.

The biggest reason is that he has made such a tremendous contribution to civic life in Utah Valley. He was instrumental in organizing the valley's first United Fund, has been a great strength to the Boy Scout movement and a dozen others.

We at KSL consider George Jedenoff a valued personal friend. We are sorry to see him go, but wish him all success, and look forward to a pleasant and valuable association with his successor.

UTAH VALLEY'S 'CAN DO' MAN GEORGE JEDENOFF

With the news that George Jedenoff will be leaving Utah Valley to take over the enormous task of running one of the nation's largest industrial complexes, United States Steel's Gary Works, I am certain everyone in the Valley is filled with mixed emotions, sadness at his leaving, and pride that one of our own would be given such a great responsibility.

Many compliments will be paid Mr. Jedenoff by the time he officially departs, but I think the best way to compliment Mr. Jedenoff is to act on the principles he worked so hard to establish.

In evaluating the substance of Mr. Jedenoff's contribution to Utah Valley, I submit that this concept best exemplifies his philosophy. With Mr. Jedenoff, the philosophy, "People Make the Difference" isn't just an abstract profoundity. He acted! The "Errors Zero" program is a good example. In this act he touched the lives, directly and indirectly, of every person in Utah Valley and many beyond the mountains of this valley. We must also consider individual cases. Mr. Jedenoff was just as concerned about individuals as he was for the group. In other words, all the way along the continuum Mr. Jedenoff was concerned and did something to make things better.

What are the rewards? Satisfaction in knowing a contribution was made, the appreciation of those benefited, advancement in ones vocation, etc.? Yes, of course. But I think the most lasting reward for Mr. Jedenoff is to succeed in bringing to realization the full potential of the programs he was so vitally interested in. The "Errors Zero" program; the United Fund; the Boy Scouts; the Utah Valley Industrial Development Association, to name a few.

If we really want to say thanks, Mr. Jedenoff, we must see to it that his "People Make the Difference" philosophy is a permanent past of the attitude of Utah Valley. From Lehi to Elberta and from the "can do" men at Geneva to the "can do" men in every other business in the valley there must be an "Errors Zero" effort.

By Richard J. Benson

SALT LAKE TRIBUNE
June 30, 1967

BYU Ceremony Honors Geneva Steel Executive

Special to The Tribune

PROVO — Gov. Calvin L. Rampton signed a proclamation in Wilkinson Center on Brigham Young University campus Thursday evening proclaiming Friday George A. Jedenoff Appreciation Day.

The governor signed the official proclamation at a banquet honoring Mr. Jedenoff for his 7½ years' leadership in Utah industry as superintendent of Geneva Steel Works. About 500 persons attended.

Leaves for Indiana

Mr. Jedenoff will leave Utah next week to become general superintendent of U.S. Steel's Gary Works in Gary, Ind.

Gov. Rampton praised Mr. Jedenoff for his efforts at Geneva despite its handicapping distance from major steel consuming markets. The 550 persons in attendance also heard Dr. Ernest L. Wilkinson, president of Brigham Young University, give a brief history of Mr. Jedenoff's life from his birth in Russia, July 3, 1917, his flight to America, years at Stanford University to his position of prominence at Geneva.

Extends LDS Thanks

Representing President N. Eldon Tanner, second counselor in the First Presidency, Church of Jesus Christ of Latter-day Saints, Victor L. Brown, second counselor in the LDS Presiding Bishopric, read a letter from President Tanner expressing appreciation from the church for Mr. Jedenoff's integrity of leadership as Geneva's superintendent.

Provo Mayor Verl Dixon was the last speaker.

The Stanford Medal

Created in 2005, the spirit and purpose of the Stanford Medal is to honor volunteer leaders who have demonstrated decades of distinguished and significant service to the University. The Stanford Medals were presented by Leslie Hume, AM '71, PhD '79, Chair of the Board of Trustees, during the Stanford Associates Award Ceremony to three dedicated alumni.

Young J. Boozer, III, '71,

has an impressive record of service for Stanford. He has served on the Board of Trustees, chaired the Alumni Association's Board of Directors, and served as the vice chair for the CUE Campaign. Passionate about Stanford, Young is known for his keen intellect and the warmth and liveliness he brings to every committee, task force, board and volunteer committee he serves on.

George A. Jedenoff, '40,

MBA '42, has been devoting prodigious amounts of enthusiasm, time, and support to various efforts at Stanford for the past 70 years. He has been a notable class leader for many years, served as a member of the Stanford Associates Board of Governors and is currently a member of the Cardinal Society Steering Committee. He constantly inspires and energizes all around him, and has clearly made volunteering for Stanford a lifelong endeavor.

Beverly Ryder, '72, has held

numerous key volunteer roles at Stanford over the past three decades. She has served on the Board of Trustees, led class reunion efforts, and served on the Stanford Alumni Association's Board of Directors becoming the second woman and first African American to chair the board. She is now on the School of Education's Advisory Committee. Beverly brings her enthusiasm and passion for Stanford to every task she undertakes.

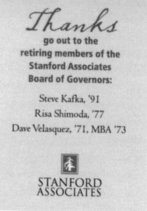

Thanks
go out to the retiring members of the Stanford Associates Board of Governors:

Steve Kafka, '91
Risa Shimoda, '77
Dave Velasquez, '71, MBA '73

STANFORD ASSOCIATES

CALVIN L. RAMPTON
GOVERNOR

STATE OF UTAH
OFFICE OF THE GOVERNOR
SALT LAKE CITY

D E C L A R A T I O N

WHEREAS, the United States Steel Company's Geneva Works is one of the great industries in Utah; and

WHEREAS, George A. Jedenoff, General Superintendent, has provided dedicated leadership and devoted efforts which have contributed greatly to the growth and strengthened position of the Geneva Works; and

WHEREAS, Mr. Jedenoff has devoted untold hours of his own time in the civic, cultural and economic development of Utah and Utah County; and

WHEREAS, the Errors Zero Program, initiated by Mr. Jedenoff and the employees of the Geneva Plant, has been highly successful and brought national attention to the plant; and

WHEREAS, the people of Utah recognize these many contributions:

NOW, THEREFORE, I, Calvin L. Rampton, Governor of the State of Utah, do hereby declare Friday, June 30, 1967, as

GEORGE A. JEDENOFF APPRECIATION DAY

in this state and urge all residents to make this a day of recognition of these contributions. I further encourage all citizens of Utah County to continue the spirit of cooperation for industrial growth as fostered by Mr. Jedenoff. On behalf of the people of the State of Utah I extend best wishes for your continued success.

Governor

AIST
Life Member
✦ GEORGE A. JEDENOFF

After graduating from Polytechnic High School of San Francisco, George A. Jedenoff graduated from Stanford in 1940, magna cum laude, with an A.B. degree in engineering. He was elected into Phi Beta Kappa and also into Tau Beta Pi, an honorary engineering association. He attended the Graduate School of Business, receiving an M.B.A. degree in 1942. He served for three years in the U.S. Navy during WWII, mostly in the Pacific Theater.

Mr. Jedenoff was employed with United States Steel Corporation for 34 years in various operations and engineering capacities. He served as general superintendent at three steel plants: Pittsburg (Calif.), Geneva Steel Works (Provo, Utah) and U. S. Steel's largest plant, Gary Steel Works, ultimately serving as vice president of operations and retiring in 1974 as president of USS Engineers and Consultants, a subsidiary. He was then hired by Kaiser Steel Corp. as president for three years to direct the company while conducting a major modernization of its Fontana, Calif., facilities. In 1977, he served as president of the Association of Iron and Steel Engineers (AISE). After retiring from Kaiser Steel, he continued to serve as a consultant to Kaiser Steel and many others, such as Kaiser Engineers, Bethlehem Steel Co., Judson Steel Co., Oregon Steel Co., Bechtel Corp., Envirotech Corp. and Southern Pacific Co.

A lifetime volunteer for Stanford, Mr. Jedenoff was on the board of governors of Stanford Associates and in 2003 was given a special award by The Associates for "an unprecedented six decades of distinguished service to Stanford" — the only such recognition ever given; in 2009 he was awarded the prestigious Stanford Medal. He has also received many other honors and distinctions for professional, educational and civic accomplishments. He is listed in Marquis Who's Who in the World and Who's Who in America. He enjoys golf and is an ardent skier, even at age 94.

Iron & Steel Technology: When and how did you first hear about AIST/AISE? Was there someone who introduced you to the association?

George Jedenoff: In 1948, after World War II, I had returned to the Pittsburg, Calif., plant of U. S. Steel and was appointed general foreman of the new cold reduction facility being built at this location. Our chief engineer, Bill Marshall, was an experienced old-timer who had been brought to California from our Eastern operations. Bill thought that establishing a local chapter of AISE would be helpful in the training of the many new engineers who were assigned to this facility. Through Bill's guidance, a chapter was established, and it proved to be very valuable in helping to train our personnel.

I&ST: What was your first level of involvement in the organization? How did your involvement progress over the years?

G.J.: As a new member of AISE, I participated in the various programs that were held at the local level. In later years, as I was transferred to a number of different locations, I continued to participate in AISE. Ultimately, in approximately 1972, I was elected to the board of AISE, advancing through the various chairs, as is customary, and finally to president in 1977. In 1983, after I had retired, I was appointed as advisor to the AISE Executive Committee and to Herschel Poole, the managing director at that time. I served in this part-time position for approximately four years, serving as a liaison with the four West Coast chapters of AISE and helping them in developing programs and securing technical speakers for their meetings.

I&ST: Have you served on any technical committees? In what role?

G.J.: I have never served on any of the technical committees of AISE, though I played a role in suggesting candidates for many of the committees. Throughout the years, I participated as the principal speaker at many local chapter meetings and regional conventions of AISE, and even delivered a technical paper on energy as part of the GEM Committee of the Iron & Steel Society of AIME in Washington, D.C.

I&ST: How has membership benefited you in your career?

G.J.: I think my membership in AISE was helpful to me in my progress through the various positions I held in the steel industry; I think that not only the technical knowledge received, but the association with so many people in the steel industry was very helpful. There were many times, in my experience, when I needed some help or to "tag base" on some decisions I had to make, and having the benefit of developing friends throughout the steel industry was most helpful in this regard. This is all a two-way street, and I am happy to report that I was able to be of help to a number of people throughout the industry who had called upon me for advice.

I&ST: How have you seen the industry change over the years?

G.J.: During my 70+ years of being associated with the steel industry, I saw many changes. The extensive introduction of computers into the various technical and managerial aspects of operations was one of the leading reasons for so many changes. But in final analysis, it's the combination of people, technology and equipment that still constitute the principal aspects of successful steel operations.

I&ST: If you were to recommend AIST to a new graduate just coming into the industry, what would you tell him/her?

G.J.: I think participation in AIST activities is extremely valuable, particularly to new graduates. The steel industry is much smaller, and there are fewer outside sources which can be utilized in becoming proficient in the more specialized activities of the steel industry. AIST is the only organization that can provide necessary technical and managerial help for new members coming into this great industry.

◆

57 YEAR
AIST Life Member

SENIORS

Local Nonagenarian Still Takes to the Slopes

By BOBBIE DODSON
Staff Writer

A legend in his own time, Orinda's George Jedenoff was chosen as a poster personality for Ski Utah. Yes, although he'll turn 96 on July 5, he still takes to those mountains, skiing with a grace that makes others on the hill take notice.

This spring, Jedenoff was treated to an all expense paid trip to Utah where he was filmed and interviewed by Ski Utah in a promo encouraging seniors to continue skiing. "One fellow followed me down the runs with three cameras," he says. "I'm told the YouTube video early on had 11,000 hits." Featured by the Alta Ski Resort, Jedenoff also appeared on local television.

This nonagenarian keeps in shape by exercising each morning before breakfast. "I'm very disciplined in doing this on the five machines I have in my basement. I have to keep fit if I want to continue skiing. My equipment was mostly given to me by others who didn't use it. Nothing is fancy; the important thing is to use it," Jedenoff explains.

He started skiing in 1960 while living in Utah and learned from the best, Alf Engen, Junior Bonous and Earl Miller, who is the granddaddy of release bindings. "Miller demonstrated how his bindings released by showing photos of himself making some sensational falls," Jedenoff says. "One day he paid me quite a compliment by remarking, 'George, you have made some falls that I have never seen before.' Now, I can ski for three weeks without having a fall. It's too hard to get up," he adds.

"With or without falls, I grew to love Alta's powder skiing, and if there is some between two trees, I'll go there," says Jedenoff. "Again, I don't need high tech equipment. I've had my boots for 20 years." When Jedenoff was transferred to Indiana in 1967, he was honored for his community service in Utah, and to lure him back, he was presented with a Lifetime Season Pass to Alta. It worked. These days he says it's

CONTRIBUTED PHOTO
At 95-years-young, George Jedenoff still enjoys skiing and lots of other activities.

easier for him to catch a plane to ski in Utah than to drive to the Lake Tahoe region – and the powder is better. His family owns a condo at Snowbird, Utah.

During the off season, Jedenoff plays golf and walks almost daily with his wife of 70 years, Barbara, in their Glorietta neighborhood. The couple moved to Orinda in 1974, but he traces his roots to Petrozavodsk, Russia where he was born in 1917. His parents were of Russian nobility. The revolution forced them to leave their homeland, first to Harbin, China, and then to the United States in 1923 where they began life anew after losing most all their material possessions. The five members of his family were granted U.S. citizenship in 1928. Jedenoff became an Eagle Scout, worked his way through Stanford University and served in the Navy in Hawaii and Guam before beginning his professional career in the steel industry. He rose to the office of president of U.S. Steel. It was after his retirement from there that Kaiser Steel tapped him to serve as president in their Oakland office in '74.

When asked to advise others aspiring to

[SEE JEDENOFF page 18]

♦ JEDENOFF *from page 17*

stay fit in their 90s, George says "Eat sensibly, don't smoke, exercise - watch yourself. I believe in moderation in all things. And try to find ways to truly enjoy life, such as skiing the slopes at Alta."

This Man Just Celebrated His 100th Birthday by Shredding Utah Powder

by Rich Stoner | 08/03/2017

There is something about longevity that fascinates me, something competitive, like you are defeating time. You have to have the focus, the drive...the luck to withstand all the pitfalls that life throws at you and impressively persevere into your 80's, 90's and even 100's. There is something equally as captivating about skiing, strapping two composite planks to your feet and schussing at high speeds down a snow filled mountain exhilarates the mind and body.

When I first heard George Jedenoff's story, I was captivated. Here was a man who was, pretty much, living out my dream by still skiing, and skiing well I might add, at the ripe old age of 99. George started skiing rather late in life at the age of 43 but swears to this day that it was the best decision that he's ever made. Since that time, this northern California native has made it a point to ski the Wasatch Mountains of Alta and Snowbird, Utah every year. In fact, the people at Ski Utah have found his story so inspiring that they have been documenting it with movies for the past five years and the most recent of which, entitled Happiness, was honored at the recent Wasatch Mountain Film Fest.

Now, with 100 on the horizon, George Jedenoff plans celebrate his birthday on July 5th by skiing with his Ski Utah friends at Snowbird. I recently caught up with Jedenoff to learn more of his inspiring story and find out how skiing has given him the happiness and drive he has needed to reach the century mark.

In one of the Ski Utah videos, you mention that beginning to ski in your 40's was one of the smartest decisions you've ever made, can you elaborate on why?

It got me started skiing. That's been my lifelong love and interest. Had I not started at that age I wouldn't have gained all the pleasure that I have had all these years. The fact that I did gave me the excitement for these years.

What role has skiing played in your longevity? How does it motivate you?

It encouraged me to exercise and without my daily exercise routine, I don't think I would've lasted this long. It's something to look forward to. I only ski about two or three days a season now. I still want to be able to handle those two or three days and that encourages me to continue my program.

You have spoken about the connection between staying in shape and still being able to ski, what is your exercise program like?

It's a little bit of everything. It's mostly to exercise my legs, back and stomach. Those are the fundamentals for skiing. It isn't the quality of the equipment it's the fact that you use it. Instead of barbells you can use cans of soup. It's something to resist your action. I don't do any of these things for a long time. I don't know if experts tell you if that works but, what the hell, it works for me. When I feel tired, I go just a little bit longer and stop. I do a lot of stretching. For skiing, I do ankle and knee work. A forward lean. Leaning forward and down so that you can get your quads to start hurting. I have an elliptical machine that a friend of mine gave me. I do about 20-30 revolutions and your quads start complaining after 10. That's wonderful for skiing. I also have one of those elastic bands that sticks in your door jamb. You can get a real workout for your upper body with that. I've got a regular step machine too. Oh yeah, a neighbor of mine bought a nordic track, one of the old ones with the oak. He was going to throw it away and asked me if I want it so I said sure. I use that every day. I picked up things in the military, high school and reading things and what other people say and put them all together. The idea is to keep going. I have a deck by my house and then several times a week I run around that thing. It's about a quarter mile. I go and when I start breathing heavy I stop. I don't a want to get a heart attack. The important thing is that you do it. The secret is that you have to make it part of your routine. Just like you brush your teeth and shave and then I go down a do my routine and have my breakfast. You just feel better.

How does skiing bring enjoyment to your life and what role does that enjoyment play in you reaching the century mark?

It's an event that I enjoy. I look forward to the challenge. It's getting back to nature. It's using the forces of nature, which is gravity. You put all those things together and It's a challenge because every little turn is different. I don't like packed slopes so much. They're okay. The thing I like to do is ski in areas where there are trees because the powder stays so much nicer around the trees. They say that I ski kind of fast on the packed slopes but you don't ski as fast in the powder, but it is tough on your legs. It's just the challenge. It's totally getting away from the problems of the world and you're just out there skiing. The fresh air in your lungs. It just makes you feel great. Because of that it's an enjoyable sport.

What are some of your best tips to live a long and prosperous life like you have?

Skiing helps me stay in shape and staying in shape leads to my longevity. Health challenges along the way have kept me alive and I'm grateful for it. I had lost about 40 pounds due to an illness and I was just skin and bones and I looked terrible in the mirror. That is when I intensified my exercise program. That has motivated me to get in shape. I watch what I eat. Don't try to eat too much. Don't eat greasy foods. Although I love desserts. I never pass those up. I don't drink any alcohol any more. I never really drank too much anyway. Take what you get.

What role do your friends and family play in motivating you to keep going?

They're doing a little more exercise watching me. They are very supportive. My son lives about three hours away and my daughter lives about 30 minutes away. I've got the four nicest grandkids and three great-grandsons with a great granddaughter to be born tomorrow. They are very supportive. You know it's interesting. Skiing is something that I enjoyed as a byproduct. I taught the kids and grandkids how to ski. I've had a whole other career but skiing has stayed with me. All the rest of it is gone and forgotten. It's the way life is. You take what you get. Don't belabor the problems that you've got. You just do what you can.

Describe for us your "powder philosophy" and the connection that it has to your positive attitude.

Powder is more challenging than a packed slope. Unless you are a skier you don't know the difference between the two. The inner mountain snow in the Wasatch is a quality of snow all by itself. The philosophy is that you enjoy that and it just brightens your day. Again it's the challenge. My friend Junior Bounous, the great hall of fame skier who is 92, he and I have skied together for 51 years. He was head of the ski school at Snowbird until he retired. He's in great shape. He's encouraged me a lot and taught me a lot of technique to handle any kind of conditions in snow. One day, he and I were going down a packed slope and he says, "George, follow me," and goes off to the side into a bunch of crud. I mean it was crud! I said, "Junior what are you doing? What are we going off here for?" He says, "All day's aren't going to be beautiful like this. All days' aren't going to have snow like this over here and are you going to sit there and mope about the fact that the ski conditions aren't good today or are you going to go out and learn how to handle this and enjoy it?" So he showed me how to handle it and pretty soon I was going through it with no problem. That's kind of a philosophical thing and powder is kind of the same. Powder is not easy to handle and it's hard on your quads and you can get tired. But if you're skiing right you don't get tired...but I get tired. Hahaha

What do you consider your best characteristic?

I never give up. And that's my worst enemy. You've got to learn when to give up. Sometimes you've got to. The challenge is knowing to give up when you should. In most people, your strongest characteristic is your biggest enemy.

As you approach 100 years old, do you see skiing as more of an opportunity or a challenge?

A pleasure. (laughs) A pleasure. I just wish that I could do it more often. I wouldn't want to do it every day. There are other things in life that are too important. It's like, you love dessert but you wouldn't want to eat dessert all the time and nothing else. That's what is really is. It's dessert. It's what you look forward to and a little of it goes a long way.

What are some of your fondest ski memories?

20 years ago on my 80th birthday I went with a group of guys and wives to New Zealand because July is their winter. On my exact birthday, July 5th, I went helicopter skiing and made four runs in the Arrowsmith range, near Christ Church, New Zealand. That was pretty exciting. It was a beautiful day and that was pretty exciting. But, I've had a lot of them. I went to Stanford and they had a group started by some professors that met every year and would go somewhere for a week or 10 days. I skied with them for 25 years and we skied all over Europe. We've just had a great deal of fellowship and wonderful friendly relations.

100-year-old skier shares 4 secrets of long, healthy, happy life

July 10, 2017, 10:12 AM EDT / Source: TODAY

By A. Pawlowski

George Jedenoff can't believe he's 100 years old and if you watch his birthday party, you'll agree. He marked the big day this month by skiing in the summer snow.

"I couldn't find a better present on my 100th birthday," Jedenoff, who has been whooshing down mountains for 57 years, told a crowd of fans gathered on the slopes of the Snowbird ski resort in Utah.

The energetic, iPhone-carrying centenarian has a youthful spirit that set the tone when a TODAY reporter addressed him as Mr. Jedenoff: "My name is George," he said right away, preferring less formality.

Born in Russia on July 5, 1917, Jedenoff came to the U.S. in 1923 after his family fled the Russian Revolution and settled on the West Coast. He graduated from Stanford University, where he met his wife, "the most important thing in my life," he said. They married in 1943.

He learned to ski in 1960, when he moved to Utah for a job transfer.

"I thought, what do people do here? They said, 'We have bowling, bridge — and a lot of people ski' and I said, that sounds like a wonderful thing to me," he told TODAY. "I took it up at age 43 and it was one of the smartest decisions that I've ever made."

He's been coming to ski in the Wasatch Mountains of Utah every year since.

What keeps him going? Here are his four rules for a good, long, healthy life:

1. Love

Jedenoff and his wife have been married for 74 years. "She is the best thing that ever happened to me in my whole life," he said.

Now 94, his wife has Alzheimer's disease and lives in a nursing home about 10 miles from the couple's house in the San Francisco Bay area. Jedenoff heads there at every lunch- and dinner-time to help feed her.

"I just feel so fortunate that I still have her and it's not a chore, it's a blessing to be able to pay her back for all the wonderful things that she's helped me with all my life."

2. Exercise

For the last 30 years, Jedenoff has made it a priority to exercise every single morning.

"My secret, if you want to call it that, is to make that part of your daily living, not a thing you sometimes do," he noted. "I get up, brush my teeth, shave and go right down and exercise, and then I have my breakfast. If you do that, you won't talk yourself out of it."

He uses some "junky equipment" in his home to work out, but it's not important what kind of equipment you have — the main goal is to work your muscles with resistance training, he said. Jedenoff does exercises for his legs, arms, abs and back. He also gets his heart pumping with the help of a few cardio machines or by jogging on his patio. His daily routine takes about 45 minutes.

3. Living in moderation

Jedenoff watches what he eats, tries not to overindulge and avoids rich, greasy foods. He no longer drinks alcohol. The centenarian loves desserts, but monitors that habit, too.

George Jedenoff learned to ski in 1960 at the age of 43. Brandon Ott / Ski Utah

4. Remembering life's priorities

Make sure to balance your life and include meaning as well as pleasure, Jedenoff advised.

"People say, 'How do you like skiing?' and I say, I love skiing but skiing is like dessert. You've got to have your main course — and that's your life. There are so many things in life you have to do and then you have your dessert and you get to ski," he said.

"Life is short, even if you go to 100 years. You have to spend time doing constructive things. Try to utilize your life for something important; try to do something good for someone else — that's wonderful therapy in itself.

"Don't live for yourself, live for the fact that you're so fortunate to be on this Earth and make use of the resources the good Lord has given you."

Made in the USA
Monee, IL
10 July 2020